W9-CEG-563

What theologians and pro-life leaders are saying about
Their Blood Cries Out...

"It was bloodguilt that brought me to the foot of the cross and the tender love of Jesus that restored my soul. *Their Blood Cries Out* is an excellent exposition of justice and mercy. Please read this book and pass it on. It deserves – no it demands to be studied."

◆**Norma McCorvey**
the former Jane Roe of Roe v. Wade

"Listen to the message of this book, and it will change the fabric of your thought about abortion, and about who is responsible for it!"

◆**Fr. Frank Pavone**
National Director, Priests for Life
President, National Pro-life Religious Council

"Justice for the innocent, the helpless, and the oppressed is an inescapable Biblical imperative. This is made abundantly, passionately, and vividly clear in *Their Blood Cries Out*. Thus, if you are unprepared for the convictions of substantive truth and the compulsion of selfless love, by all means do not read this book. It is that powerful, that persuasive, and that provocative."

◆**George Grant, Ph.D.**
Director, King's Meadow Study Center
and author of over four dozen books, including
Grand Illusions: The Legacy of Planned Parenthood

"Every once in awhile, it does you good to read a book that makes your blood boil. *Their Blood Cries Out* is that book!"

◆**Joe Schiedler**
National Director Pro-Life Action League

"This book is so powerful that it can change your life! <u>It changed mine!</u>"

◆**Fr. Timothy Hopkins**
St. Philomena, Miami, Florida

"This is a heaven-breathed prophetic warning in our present national crisis, where the Abortion Holocaust has continued in the United States for three decades. God hears the cries of the unavenged innocent blood shed in our land, and in spite of His longsuffering, He promises to judge nations whose laws and institutions fail to protect innocent life from slaughter. The salt has lost its savor and has not preserved the standard of God's law and grace in society without which there can be no peace. We have chosen apathy over love, comfort over sacrifice, and as a result, the gavel of God's wrath is lifted above us, ready to fall. But there is hope, there is a blood that speaks better things than that of Abel, and Newman shows us the way. Troy Newman's monument is a call to judge ourselves, lest we be judged. It is an encouraging exhortation to all who labor to protect the innocent and end the legalized child-killing. It is a roadmap to all who dream of salvation in America and who long to see God's wrath abated and His favor bestowed upon us once again. "

◆**Patrick Johnston, D.O.**
Family Practice, Zanesville, Ohio

Their Blood Cries Out

By
Troy Newman
with
Cheryl Sullenger

Foreword by Rev. Joseph Foreman
Co-founder, Operation Rescue

Preface by Fr. Frank Pavone,
National Director, Priests for Life

RESTORATION PRESS
Wichita, Kansas

OPERATION RESCUE WEST

P.O. Box 601150
Sacramento, CA 95860
www.operationrescue.org

Restoration⊕press

P.O. Box 781045
Wichita, KS 67278-1045

Cover art by Mitch Irion
www.creativewing.com

ISBN: 0-9720367-5-x

For Scott Olafson,

Who lived the life of a Rescuer, who died the death of a Rescuer, whose innocent blood was spilled upon the land, and whose voice now cries out from under the altar of God in unity with the children he endeavored to rescue. May the Blood that speaks a better word than that of Abel answer Scott's cries for justice.

Contents

Acknowledgments

$\mathcal{T}$his is the second edition of *Their Blood Cries Out*, and I am pleased to note that it contains substantial differences from the first printing. The first edition was our maiden voyage into the world of publishing. Because of the life-and-death nature of the subject matter, (for the pre-born, at least), it was rushed into print before many of the wrinkles could be smoothed. Much was learned from that first endeavor, and this edition stands corrected and improved on many levels because of that experience. It is our hope and prayer that its message touches the hearts and changes the lives of those who read it.

As I mentioned in the previous edition, the creation of this book is a direct result of my work in the pro-life movement over the last decade or more. The contents are a sum of the great teachings from my pastors, leaders, co-labors, and committed individuals who have shared biblical insights with me throughout my relatively short tenure as a Christian ministering on the streets of America. This book is the outcome of positive Christian discipleship from many persons who have taken the time to train me in the ways of Christianity. Thank you.

I must again thank Pastor Gary Cass for charging me with the writing of this book. Had he not looked me in the eye and told me to write, this book would have ended up on my eternal pile of "good projects" left uncompleted.

Many people have spent hours of work providing valuable insights. Notable among those are Rev. Joseph

Foreman, Dr. Patrick Johnston, and Dr. Don Smith. Others spent equally long hours proofreading and editing, including Marcie Northum, Allyson Smith, and Nellie Meyers. Without the contributions of these people, this book would not have been possible.

Cheryl Sullenger's contributions to this book are endless. Suffice it to say that she was able to turn transient thoughts and incoherent phrases into something resembling literature. I am very grateful for her commitment to the babies, her word processing talent, and theological wisdom.

Four years ago, I began to pray for a renewed broken heart. I had been viewing the pictures of aborted children with a callous eye and speaking on their behalf with an indifferent voice. The LORD answered my prayer by shattering my spirit. Today, I cannot gaze upon the lifeless bodies or speak about the tragedy of child-killing without being moved nearly to tears.

Certainly, this humble work was derived from my deeply held belief that abortion is a most savage act of violence. I am persuaded that God has a critical message for us today concerning this wanton shedding of innocent blood. It is a message that desperately cries out from the blood of aborted children of the need for dramatic changes in the way we, as Christians and as a nation, think and act toward the child in the womb. *Their Blood Cries Out* endeavors to faithfully deliver that message as clearly as possible. May God bless those who read it with a fresh vigor to end the killing.

Troy Newman
June, 2003
Wichita, Kansas

Foreword

*T*here is probably no one more alienated within today's Christian community than the active pro-lifer. He is considered too narrowly focused and out of step, a zealot who impugns the reputation of all other reasonable Christians. After all, what kind of Christian would dare to hold one of those disgusting graphic photos of aborted fetuses on a public street corner? Certainly not the respectable kind. But if there is some level of toleration for those rather odd folks who take their pet issue onto the streets, it is not something that the church embraces. Their behavior, at best, is viewed as some kind of esoteric function of the body of Christ that the vast majority of Christians can politely excuse themselves from as not being their "calling."

"Not everyone is a hand or a foot," pro-lifers are often told. "You cannot expect everyone to have the same calling. We are glad that you have been called to save babies from abortion, but we have not been called to be one-issue Christians."

Herein lies the misunderstanding that is currently fragmenting the Body of Christ. Are those who take direct action to stop abortion really functioning in a subset of Christianity, in much the same category perhaps as the women's quilting clubs or the men's surfing ministry? Certainly not everyone is called to make quilts for charity or evangelize the surfer-dude crowd while catching a few waves down at Tourmaline Park in San Diego. In the same way, not everyone is called to save babies from abortion. Right?

This kind of thinking could not be more wrong. It is

completely contrary to the picture of who and what a Christian is as defined by the Bible. There are certain behaviors that are required by God of all Christians, regardless of their "calling" or ministry. For a Christian to exhibit the fullness of what it means to be a follower of Christ he must:

- ◆ Read God's Word regularly
  (Deuteronomy. 6:6-9)
- ◆ Pray regularly
  (1 Thessalonians 5:17)
- ◆ Attend church regularly
  (Hebrews 10:25)
- ◆ Love his fellow man, especially other Christians
  (Matthew 22:39, 1 John 3:10)
- ◆ Treat others as he would like to be treated
  (Matthew 7:12)

These are the key aspects of traditional, authentic Christianity, and are to be apparent in every one who names the name of Christ. These define a Christian and are natural expressions of faith that flow from willing and grateful hearts as fruit of the Holy Spirit that now indwells him.

Imagine one Christian telling another, "I have the gift of church attendance, but not the gift of Bible reading. I thank God that you have been called to read your Bible, but that does not mean that I must. After all, we are all different members of the body." There is some small shred of truth in this ludicrous statement since not all will be able to quit their jobs and devote their lives to Bible study. Some have but does this make them zealots and fanatics that respectable Christians should hold at an arm's length? More importantly, does the fact that some become full-time Bible scholars absolve the rest of Christians from reading God's Word?

As illogical as that sounds, this position parallels what is being expressed to those who take seriously the Biblical mandate articulated in the Parable of the Good Samaritan, Proverbs 24:11-12, and elsewhere in the Scriptures. This mandate commands that Christians first rescue, then render meaningful assistance to the innocent who are threatened with imminent death. Yet Christians who actively obey this mandate tend to be marginalized, dismissed, and rudely disrespected by their brothers and sisters in Christ. But what is worse, the innocent babies for whom they are advocates, that are scheduled to die at our local abortion clinics, are ignored by the church and heartlessly left to their cruel fates.

To understand why this is happening, we must first understand the root cause of our attitudes about abortion. This cannot be done without understanding the doctrine of bloodguilt. Because of the state-sanctioned murder of millions of innocent children created in the image of God, all of us are affected by bloodguilt. This causes us to want to avoid the issue of abortion because it brings us the uncomfortable feeling that all is not right. We may not even be able to verbalize this discomfort, but it is there nonetheless. Those who insist on bringing up the issue, especially those who encourage others to take direct action to stop abortion, are repelled in attempts to get rid of those guilty feelings that plague us. However, once we face the issue of bloodguilt, discover what the Bible says about it, and what the remedies are for it, we can appropriately apply God's Word and be finally loosed from the guilt that now oppresses us.

It must be understood that the authors of this book are not looking for activists to join a movement, a cause, or an organization. Activism, in and of itself, is not the answer to abortion or any other problem. However, once a person becomes a Christian, part of his duty as such is to pattern his life after Christ and His teachings. This includes the obedience to the commandment to love his neighbor as he loves himself – even his pre-born neighbor.

> *We know that we have come to know him if we obey his commands. The man who says, "I know him," but does not do what he commands is a liar, and the truth is not in him. But if anyone obeys his word, God's love is truly made complete in him. This is how we know we are in him: Whoever claims to live in him must walk as Jesus did* (1 John 2:3-6).

There is no attempt in this book to reduce Christianity to a laundry list of items that once completed, add up to a formula for righteousness. In fact, quite to the contrary, this book does attempt to help Christians to act like Christians whose obedient behavior is simply a natural expression of their faith. 1 John 2:5 says, *"But if anyone obeys his word, God's love is truly made complete in him."*

Christianity is inherently pro-life. Once believers come to understand the unavoidable responsibility bestowed upon them by God to rescue the innocent, they will instinctively know what to do about it. Even if they cannot become full time pro-life workers, and few will, they will gladly and obediently make time in their lives to reach out and rescue the innocent, just as they find time to read the Scriptures, pray, and attend church services.

Unfortunately, today's Christians lack teaching on the doctrines of innocent blood and bloodguilt. Since they do not understand the problem, they cannot recognize the biblical solution. Thus, the uncomfortable subject of abortion continues to be avoided by the church, babies continue to die, and the guilt continues.

Their Blood Cries Out is an attempt to change that. It clearly and concisely lays out the Biblical teaching on the matter of innocent bloodshed and what our responsibilities are as Christians not only to stop it, but to lead our nation in repentance so that God will bring healing and restoration to a nation aching under the curse of bloodguilt. It is a work of love because love for God and for our fellow man regardless of age or stage of development demands no less.

Rev. Joseph Foreman
Co-founder, Operation Rescue

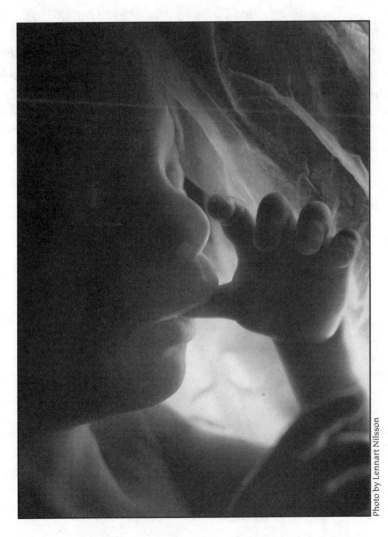

A child in the womb at five months gestation.

Preface

Many believers will say that the first spiritual response we should have to the tragedy of abortion is prayer.

I disagree.

The first, and foundational, spiritual response to the tragedy of abortion must be repentance. As God makes clear in the first chapter of Isaiah, He cannot hear the prayers of unrepentant people whose hands are full of blood. And like it or not, the blood of aborted children is on our hands.

Troy Newman traces, by means of this book, why that is true, and how it is that God can ask us to repent of evil deeds that we did not even do! While our hands may not have reached in to dismember these children, the fact remains that whenever innocent blood is shed upon the land, it implicates everyone in the land. Shed blood splashes on us all, and when that happens, we simply cannot look the other way.

That, in fact, is the other side of the tragedy of abortion. The first aspect of the tragedy is that it happens; the second is that while it happens, so many go on with life "business as usual." They think abortion is just "an issue," and worse, they think it's an issue they can choose not to deal with. They have the mistaken notion, often reinforced by the silence of the pulpit, that somehow the fight against abortion is something they can join up with if they want, but if they are not so inclined, it is all right to let others handle it.

When I first came to the conviction in 1993 that I could not go on "business as usual" with my own life unless I devoted every ounce of my time and energy to ending abortion, some of my friends, in a very well-meaning way, told me they were happy that I was going to be able "to do my thing." I corrected them. It's not "my thing." We don't get into the fight against abortion because we are attracted to it, or because it's some kind of hobby.

Abortion is a worldwide emergency, and threatens the very fabric of civilization. There is no such thing as a choice "not to be involved" in this war. We are all involved, and as this book makes clear, our response to abortion shapes our very relationship with God.

It has been said that he who would change the world must change the very fabric of his own thinking. If you listen closely to the message of this book, it will change the fabric of your thinking about abortion, and it will enable you to put into practice the fruits of repentance. I give thanks to God not only for the message of this book, but for the Lord's servant who wrote it, a man who has not hesitated to cry out for the truth across this land. I am proud to join hands with him and so many like him who have heard the summons, and having heard it, know that life can never be the same again. Their blood cried out!

Fr. Frank Pavone
National Director, Priests for Life
President, National Pro-life Religious Council

Introduction

The wrath of God is being revealed from heaven against all the godlessness and wickedness of men who suppress the truth by their wickedness, since what may be known about God is plain to them, because God has made it plain to them. For since the creation of the world God's invisible qualities—his eternal power and divine nature—have been clearly seen, being understood from what has been made, so that men are without excuse...Although they know God's righteous decree that those who do such things deserve death, they not only continue to do these very things but also approve of those who practice them.
Romans 1:18-20 & 32

Why the Angst?

The young, heavy-set woman emerged from the abortion clinic accompanied by her older friend. The cotton ball taped to the back of her hand, where the abortion clinic nurse had inserted the IV needle required before the five-minute abortion surgery, was evidence of her post-abortion state. She refused offers of literature from sidewalk counselors who stood on the sidewalk near their graphic signs of aborted children that leaned against a row of trees lining the street.

As she passed the final signs, she kicked them over and angrily swore at the Christians she had just passed. One of the Christian sidewalk counselors softly reminded her that they had offered her help before she aborted her baby, so she had no one to blame for the death of her child but herself. At this statement, the woman flew into a rage. To the surprise and distress of her friend, she turned and charged at the Christian, threatening to kill her if she spoke another word.

The sidewalk counselor again reminded her that they were there to help her and would help her even now that her baby was dead. It took three people to hold the angry woman back from fulfilling her threat upon the Christian. Eventually, after quite a disturbance, the older friend was able to take the woman who had aborted by the arm and forcibly usher her to their awaiting vehicle, while she cursed and screamed the entire way.

What is it about abortion that evokes such a powerful response?

Oddly, it can be described as both a simple five-minute operation on the one hand and as a deep, incurable wound on the other. How could it be that something so simple, even if healed, can still leave scars that remain for an eternity, so tender to the touch? And why is it that even a statement as simple and as obvious as this paragraph will provoke someone to fly apart at the seams?

We are so familiar with the powerful response of this issue that we either flee the debate, or jump into the middle of it and miss the irony of how something so simple can have such profound repercussions.

The prevalence of this simple surgery has made it so that these repercussions are impacting more and more people, families, churches and communities. Since 1973, over 41,600,000 abortions have occurred in America, based on information distributed by the Alan Guttmacher Institute, a pro-abortion research organization. Even considering the fact that many mothers have had more than one abortion, we still have a staggering third of mothers affected directly. In plain language, about a fourth of the mothers who know they are pregnant end up hiring a killer to snuff out the life of their growing child and place his broken remains in an abortionist's jar. If you could stand and watch what takes place in the procedure room, you would literally see this happen.

Now, add to those millions of moms affected by abortion an equal number of fathers. Quadruple that figure and you have the number of grandparents affected. Finally, we cannot leave out all the surviving siblings, the friends who took their companions to the abortion clinic, and the abortion clinic staff whose lives have been forever altered by a woman's right to choose. In fact, it is hard to find a person whose life has not been touched by abortion. They sit next to us in church. They are our friends. They are our pastors. They are our wives and husbands, sisters and brothers, and even our own children.

And nobody wants to talk about it.

Such a simple little operation. . .

It could be that there is *more* to it than merely removing a blob of tissue and that the guilt stems from more than pro-life rhetoric. Perhaps the moms, dads, grandparents, friends, neighbors, and clinic staffers understand the deep-reaching implications of this simple procedure more profoundly than the heated rhetoric of the most ardent pro-life imagination. Thus we see the evidence of the overwhelming sense of guilt.

But feeling guilt does not make one guilty. The questions must be asked: Are *they* guilty? Are *we* guilty? If so, of what are we guilty? What about those of us in society who have no part in anyone's abortion? If there is guilt, are there practical solutions?

For the answers, we need only to look as far as our Bibles, where God has clearly explained not only the problem of innocent bloodshed, as abortion clearly is, but also His plan for bringing restoration to a people so burdened by it. There, in the Scriptures, we find the reason for the angst surrounding abortion: Bloodguilt.

The guilt we all suffer, to varying extents, because of the murder of innocent babies through abortion is real. We believe everyone knows it is real and that is why they react the way they do. They are not over-reacting. They are simply fulfilling what Romans 1:18-20 & 32 both describes and predicts:

> *Although they know God's righteous decree*
> *that those who do such things deserve death,*
> *they not only continue to do these very things*
> *but also approve of those who practice them.*

Not only do the guilty approve of those who practice abortion, but they disapprove – sometimes violently – of those who so are so bold as to shine the light of truth upon their sinful deed.

God says we are guilty and our own hearts condemn us. One of the great problems we face is that people can become so burdened by their own guilt that they cannot believe that relief is possible, so they wither in silent self-condemnation or explode in violent anger, convinced that there is no hope while they lash out at themselves or others. Thankfully, God's Word gives us more than a hopeless guilty verdict. It gives us valid answers that can truly and completely eradicate guilt regardless of our level of involvement.

We as a nation, as individuals, but especially as Christians must stop ignoring the topic of abortion and boldly confront the biblical doctrine of bloodguilt and what it means to us today. If we are as legitimately guilty as we seem to be acting, then we must retreat to the Scriptures to find out what can be done to bring relief, forgiveness, and healing to our people and our land.

The blood of the innocent aborted babies cries out, as you will see in the following pages of this book, calling for justice and convicting the consciences of those whose hands are stained thereby. But along with it also comes the answering blood of Jesus Christ, bringing restoration through those who are willing to take up their crosses and follow in His footsteps.

Author Troy Newman and Joseph Scheidler stand outside a large church in San Diego, California, in May, 2002, urging church-goers to change their attitudes and actions concerning their pre-born neighbors.

Newman and co-author Cheryl Sullenger oppose experimentation on human embryos in December, 1999, outside the Geron Corporation in Menlo Park, California, a biotech lab that destroys live human embryos for research.

Part One:

The Problem
of
Innocent Blood

*Woe to him who builds a town
with bloodshed,
who establishes a city by iniquity!*
Habakkuk 2:12

*Also on your skirts is found
the blood of the lives of the poor innocents.
I have not found it by secret search,
but plainly on all things.*
Jeremiah 2:34

Chapter 1

Do not trust in deceptive words and say, "This is the temple of the LORD, the temple of the LORD, the temple of the LORD!" If you really change your ways and your actions and deal with each other justly, if you do not oppress the alien, the fatherless or the widow and do not shed innocent blood in this place, and if you do not follow other gods to your own harm, then I will let you live in this place, in the land I gave your forefathers for ever and ever. But look, you are trusting in deceptive words that are worthless.
Jeremiah 7:4-8

Church Life in Anytown, USA

Jessica's home pregnancy test confirmed her fears. Her heart sank as the little dot at the end of the stick transformed to a glowing red before her astonished blue eyes. Just to make sure, Jessica reached into the pack and dipped the second test-stick into her morning urine. Her heart sank as she read the inevitable results. Now there could be no doubt: Jessica was pregnant.

She wondered how this could have happened, as she sat alone behind the locked bathroom door. Jason, her boyfriend, had promised that she would not get pregnant. She felt a sting of betrayal as she remembered his words of assurance, whispered gently as he persuaded her. It was only twice: once after school at his parents' house and another

19

time during the summer while her parents were at work. She
had so trusted him with her tender heart that it just seemed
impossible that he could have been so wrong.

Jason had recently set out for college, leaving Jessica
at home to complete her final two years of high school. She
knew that they could not get married right away because she
was only sixteen years old. They spoke often together of
getting married after Jason had finished college and
established himself in his career. Somehow, talking of
marriage made having sex a little easier for Jessica. She
justified her indiscretion by convincing herself that she and
Jason were so in love that it was almost as if they were already
married but just waiting for the date and ceremony to make
it official. She thought that God would certainly understand
that their heart-commitment to one another was more
important than a few ritualistic words recited before a room
full of people.

But now the pregnancy had changed things. Jessica
anguished over how the news would disappoint her parents,
affect her schooling, and devastate her plans for the future.
As Jessica fought to control her tears and a welling sense of
panic, a name suddenly came to Jessica's mind: Susan. Jessica
had not seen Susan for several months, although she had
once been a faithful member of the church youth group where
Jessica was actively involved. Susan had told everyone that
she was spending time with her new friends and no longer
had time for the youth group, but Jessica remembered the
whispered rumors that last year Susan had quietly aborted
an unintended pregnancy after breaking up with her
boyfriend. Jessica felt confident that Susan would help her
find a way out of this problem.

Jessica was surprised to see Susan smoking a cigarette

when she picked Jessica up at the end of her street early Saturday morning. Jessica had told her mom that they had to leave early to help with preparations for the church car wash, but instead the girls were hurrying off to avoid being late for Jessica's appointment at the Planned Parenthood clinic on Main Street. Neither girl talked much during the trip downtown. Susan occupied the uncomfortable silence by fiddling with the radio tuner, finally landing on a station playing music that Jessica found obnoxious and a little vulgar. She noticed that her friend had changed and she was not sure she liked the new Susan as much as she had the old.

The two girls drove past the people standing on the sidewalk offering pamphlets to the passengers of cars entering the clinic's parking lot. Jessica covered her face with her purse when she recognized one of the leaflet-holders as a person from her church, but Susan did not seem to care.

Inside, the spacious waiting room was crowded with girls her age and some even younger. Several were with older women, others were with men, and still more were huddled in the corners pretending to read magazines. Jessica could feel the tension in the room. It was not a time for light conversation. Everyone seemed consumed with his or her own thoughts.

Jessica, although unable even to receive an aspirin from the school nurse without her parents' permission filled out all the required consent forms for anesthesia and outpatient surgery while her mother and father went about their weekend routine oblivious of what their minor daughter was about to endure. The receptionist told Jessica that if she lacked adequate funds there was no need for concern. Since their fees were based on a sliding scale, Planned Parenthood would provide the abortion at a reduced rate or even free.

Susan had already coached Jessica on how to answer all the questions correctly to avoid having to pay.

After what seemed a dreadfully long wait, Jessica's name was finally called. She quietly left her chair and accompanied the nurse to the procedure room. She was weighed and her blood pressure was checked. The nurse brusquely instructed her to strip, put on a hospital gown, and get on the table. She was injected with a light narcotic and soon slipped uneasily into "twilight sleep" where, though conscious, she remembered very little.

She was vaguely aware of the whirring of the suction machine and the hiss of the liquid in the vacuum tube, but she clearly remembered a female voice saying, "We got it all."

Jessica's youth pastor, Mike, thought that something had been bothering Jessica for the last couple of weeks. He suspected that her relationship with her boyfriend had turned too serious too quickly. When she uncharacteristically showed up late at the church car wash, Mike thought she looked pale and a little weak. He mistook her post-abortion condition for his suspicion that Jessica was suffering from morning sickness. Concerned for his normally perky charge, he waited for the right time to say something to her.

Jessica shrugged off his queries about her health and her relationship with Jason. She mentioned that she was tired from a long week of testing at school and that she missed her boyfriend, but she was trusting in God and His plan for her. As Jessica lied, her church-cliches suddenly sounded as empty and hollow as she felt in the face of her grief and sense of guilt.

Pastor Mike was inwardly relieved. Jessica's responses seemed plausible enough. He was satisfied that she was just going through the natural emotional dips and swings that typically characterize the teen-age years. With his busy schedule of balancing work, ministry, and making time for his new wife, he certainly did not need the inconvenience – or the embarrassment – of one of "his kids" getting pregnant and all the fall-out that would entail. "Besides, Jessica wouldn't lie to me," he thought.

Sharon and Steve had been married for only one year before she became pregnant with Justin. The two wanted to wait for a few years to start a family so they would be better financially prepared for the added expenses of raising children, but when Justin surprised them, Sharon quit her job and devoted her time and energies to being a good mother. Three years later they had Samuel. Steve was delighted to have two boys and felt lucky to have a wife who invested so much in their family. Everyone thought Sharon, Steve, and the boys were an ideal family.

Steve's career was taking off and he had just received a promotion, but he was spending long hours at the office. Sharon loved her sons but they were a handful and she often felt isolated and lonely. She secretly anticipated the day when she could finally put Samuel in pre-school and resume her own career.

At last, both boys were in school and Sharon went back to work at her old job. With extra money now in the budget, they purchased a larger house, two new vehicles, and other nice things that made their lives together comfortable. She began to sing in the choir on Sunday and with the worship team on Wednesday nights, which helped her meet new people and feel more connected. "Life couldn't be better!" she was often overheard saying to her friends.

More and more Steve was consumed with his career so he did not notice when Sharon began showing signs of queasiness in the mornings. Sharon had been faithfully taking the pill since she weaned Samuel. She had not bothered to mention to Steve that she had missed her last period and now she was missing her second. Life had been so busy she just ignored the missed cycle. But now she knew. She knew like any woman who has ever borne children knows. She recognized what her body was telling her and she did not need a pregnancy test to confirm her symptoms. Sharon was with child.

Sharon had had one abortion while she was still in college before she met Steve. But not a soul knew about it. It was one secret she was taking to her grave. She had justified the abortion by telling herself that she was too young, and that the child would have interfered with her education, forcing her to live in hardship. She told herself repeatedly in the following years that her decision to abort was for the best.

Sharon felt that Steve would be happy to have another child, but she was worried. They had come to depend on her salary. Steve had just bought a new Ford F150 and the payments on that, along with the mini-van and a hefty mortgage were just too much to handle on one paycheck. She did not want to give up the good things they could now afford only to go back to struggling to make ends meet. Besides, she was enjoying her career again and her renewed social life. The thought of going back to sleep-deprived nights, feeding schedules, diaper changes, weight gain, and isolation did not seem appealing. So she made up her mind. She had done it once and she could do it again. It would be for the best.

She left the boys with Steve on Saturday morning, telling him that she had some errands to run and would be back in the afternoon. With two empty car seats in the back of the mini-van she drove into the parking lot of Planned Parenthood, slowing down only long enough to shout to the anti-abortion protestors, "Judge not lest ye be judged!"

Arriving home that afternoon, Sharon peeled the Band-Aid off the back of her hand before she pulled into her driveway. The cotton gauze with one spot of her own blood was the only physical evidence left of Lady MacBeth's morning's errands. She discarded the bandage and the paperwork from Planned Parenthood into the trash receptacle and headed for bed, telling Steve not to wake her up for dinner because she had a headache.

◆ ◆ ◆

Pastor Ray was just beginning a six-month series on the book of Romans when he first met with Michelle. Now it was five months later, and she was insisting on a meeting with him as she had repeatedly since she began attending his church. Pastor Ray had apprehensions about Michelle, who always seemed to find unique and creative ways of inserting the topic of abortion into almost any conversation. Some of the other church members had complained that they thought Michelle was too pushy about her favorite subject. She wore a "little feet" pin every day and had an excessive number of pro-life bumper stickers plastered on her car. She spent her Saturdays downtown praying in front of the Planned Parenthood clinic. He tolerated these idiosyncrasies without a word since she was always quite friendly, paid close attention during services, and had kind words for his sermons. She recently volunteered to work in the Sunday school classes and, most importantly, she tithed faithfully. However, he was not looking forward to the inescapable meeting with Michelle. Pastor Ray was sure that she wanted something from him and that thing would have to do with the abortion issue. He did not like being put on the spot.

But the meeting went well. She called the following Sunday "Sanctity of Human Life Sunday" and it seemed harmless enough. It was the anniversary of the abortion decision, Roe versus Wade. Pastor Ray had been generally aware of the Supreme Court ruling, but found Michelle a veritable font of knowledge on the subject. All through the meeting Michelle kept emphasizing the fact that abortion was murder and that the Bible says it is the duty of Christians to do something about it. It seemed important to Michelle that he mention abortion from the pulpit on this all-important day. While Michelle's talk of "duty" to the unborn made Pastor Ray uncomfortable, he promised her that he would say something about the babies next Sunday. He placed his hand on her shoulder and gently ushered her toward the door, firmly assuring Michelle that the church was solidly and unequivocally pro-life.

True to his word, Pastor Ray spent about five minutes before his sermon, talking about the value of human life. As he read Jeremiah 1:5 to his fidgeting congregation, a baby near the back of the sanctuary began to cry. Pastor Ray took the opportunity to terminate the subject with a short, baby-related joke he had rehearsed just for the occasion. The audience laughed and Ray launched into Romans.

It started immediately after service. One of the more

respected women in the church, offended at what she considered inappropriate political remarks, refused to shake Pastor Ray's hand. Although one of the older men quietly commended him on his bravery for broaching the controversial subject, one of the elders took him aside to admonish him about discussing such a divisive issue in the middle of a building project.

When Pastor Ray came into the office on Tuesday, his secretary reported to him that Sunday's offering was well below normal and that there were several notes placed in the offering basket. Anonymous messages and calls sporadically plagued the church receptionist. One particularly nasty note was from a woman, Sharon, who sang in the choir. She and her husband, Steve, had tithed regularly for years. Their letter said that they would not be coming back.

On Wednesday afternoon, as Pastor Ray was re-reading Sunday's letters and notes, his youth pastor, Mike, tapped on his door and asked for a few minutes of time. The parents of a girl in the youth group had come to him for advice concerning a change of behavior in their daughter, Jessica. She had been crying and refusing to speak to her parents since Sunday. The family was distraught with concern and began to fear that Jessica may have been involved in an abortion.

Already feeling overworked and stressed by the burden of his responsibilities as the pastor of a large and growing church with a large and growing debt, Pastor Ray was simply overwhelmed by the avalanche of problems caused by such a few short – and seemingly innocuous – comments. Ray quickly made a private vow. The subject of abortion would never again be mentioned from the church pulpit as long as he was pastor.

◆◆◆

This church is representative of what could be considered an average church in America. The accounts we just related are based on true events. Similar incidents have occurred with predictable regularity in churches across our land for over thirty years. Pews are filled with women and men who have been involved in abortions. They all have their story. When the issue of abortion comes up, they tend to get upset and even angry. Sometimes they accuse others of judging them in the worst sort of way.

This reaction may seem surprising to some. Why are there such defensive and emotional responses to the common procedure of an early abortion? The procedure is ordinarily brief; an experienced abortionist can do a suction abortion in about ten minutes. Although the complications and side effects can be serious, most people are not aware of them, and that is not their objection to the topic of abortion. No, the problem is related to the suggestion that abortion takes an innocent human life. This position is controversial, political, and partisan. It inspires guilt, and the condemnation of others. It runs contrary to the current social stance that a woman should have a right to control her own reproductive destiny – to the view that what people do with their own bodies is their business.

And those involved in an abortion decision are not the only ones who object to the mention of the "A" word. The media is reticent to cover it, political candidates hesitate to discuss it, pastors refuse to preach about it, and the average man on the street does not want to think about it. When a brave soul does confront a candidate about his abortion stand or show a photo of an aborted child on a street corner, the backlash is usually tremendous. Something that is supposed to be so common and unobjectionable can provoke some of the most devastating reactions.

There is a reason for this adverse response to the topic of abortion. That reason is found throughout the Scriptures as clearly as any other basic doctrine of the faith. There is a price to pay for the shedding of innocent blood. That price is bloodguilt.

What is bloodguilt and what does the Bible say about it? How does bloodguilt affect our communities, our nations, and our churches? Does it affect those who have not experienced abortion in the same way as those who have? What is the remedy? Is there any hope?

The first section of this book will explore in detail why innocent blood is such a problem for everyone in our nation, even those who have no apparent involvement in abortion. The second part will explain the biblical doctrine of bloodguilt, which comes upon men and nations as the consequence of innocent bloodshed. In the third section we will discover who, according to the Scriptures, bears responsibility for not only the problem of bloodguilt but also for the solution. Finally, we will describe the biblical steps to restoring our nation from the devastating consequences that bloodguilt has wrought upon our people and our land.

We will find that the participation of God's people is essential in satisfying the righteous demands for justice and bringing forgiveness and restoration to our families, churches, communities, and our nation. Now is the time for the followers of Christ to stop being part of the problem, either wittingly or unwittingly, and learn to become part of the solution. This book was written for that purpose.

Chapter 2

America's Polluted Land

Listening to Peter Jennings every night one might come to the conclusion that the world is full of pollution. ABC's environmental update section of the news regularly reports on the latest breaking stories from the eco-front. On any given night we may hear of an oil spill off the coast of Mexico, a sunken nuclear submarine contaminating the ocean floor, or some mega-corporation dumping sludge into the Hudson River. When news is thin, there is always the favorite hot topic of global warming. This phenomenon, we are repeatedly told, is caused by automobile exhausts and the burning of the rain forests and is responsible for melting polar ice caps, coastal flooding, and catastrophic global weather patterns.

There is great public interest in the matter of pollution, so much so that movies dealing with this subject matter are well received at the box office. Julia Roberts won an Academy Award for her role as Erin Brokovich, a woman who single-handedly brought down a public utility mogul for poisoning the drinking water of a small California town. Likewise, John Travolta made a huge splash, not to mention a lot of money, starring in a film as a greedy personal injury lawyer-turned-hero for attempting to punish a large corporation for dumping deadly toxic waste.   These films, based on true stories, trumpet the cause of the environmentalist movement, which is bravely battling the evils of pollution, all the while ignoring the most serious form of pollution that defiles our land.

While the world looks on the outside of the cup, God says that the inside of the cup is where the true threat lies. The Bible is clear that a land may be polluted both physically and spiritually by certain acts of man. When this happens, God promises to bring His Righteous Judgment upon those nations that allow such polluting deeds. In particular, there is one toxic waste in the Bible so foul that it will cause Almighty God to reach down from Heaven to complete an environmental cleanup of Biblical proportions.

The most damaging agent to the earth's environment is **innocent blood**. The shedding of innocent blood pollutes the nation that tolerates it.

> *Do not pollute the land where you are.* <u>*Bloodshed pollutes the land*</u>*, and atonement cannot be made for the land on which blood has been shed, except by the blood of the one who shed it* (Numbers 35:33).

> *They shed innocent blood, the blood of their sons and daughters, whom they sacrificed to the idols of Canaan, and the <u>land was desecrated by their blood</u>* (Psalm 106:38).

> *Gilead is a city of wicked men, <u>stained with footprints of blood</u>* (Hosea 6:8).

God places the highest value upon human life and

when even one innocent life is wrongly taken, God objects.

The God who takes note of each sparrow that falls to the ground, is certainly aware when one created in His image is unjustly killed. The stench of the shed blood of murdered human beings rises to heaven, offending the God in whose image they were created.

But does this apply to those still in their mother's wombs? A brief look at the miraculous development of a child *in utero* shows, from a scientific perspective, that what is being aborted in our nation's hospitals and clinics is not just mere lumps of inanimate tissue, but fully human, living beings in a most remarkable stage of life.

At the moment that the woman's egg is fertilized by the sperm of the man, a new and unique individual is formed. This individual has all the genetic information that will later determine sex, physical traits, intellectual capacity and emotional makeup.

After fertilization (conception), the single cell comprising the early body of this new boy or girl begins to divide. It moves down the fallopian tube into the uterus where 5-10 days later it implants. The baby, now called an embryo, continues his rapid development. Just 18 days after conception, a tiny heart is pumping blood throughout the child's growing body. By Day 20 there is a rudimentary brain, spinal cord, and nervous system in place. At 28 days, tiny arms and legs are budding. The skeleton is formed by Day 42 and brain waves can be recorded as early as Day 43. A study from Great Britain recently determined that the growing baby is capable of experiencing pain as early as six weeks from conception. By the eighth week, the child is fully formed, possessing every organ that you and I possess.   This individual will continue to grow and mature until the reaching adulthood, sometime around eighteen years of age.

Modern technologies have greatly advanced the science of fetology. Now we can see in 4-D[1] ultrasound the most detailed pictures of the tiny baby in the womb. There can be no doubt, from a scientific perspective, that the occupant of the pregnant uterus is a human being. Today, one fourth[2] of all healthy American children who come to temporarily reside in the cozy confines of the uterus will find it made purposely inhospitable. Mother's womb has become a death-chamber. There can be only one word to accurately describe the intentional death of this human life during an abortion. That word is *murder.*

Some non-biblically based ethicists try to dance around the issue of murder by claiming that it cannot be known with any certainty when sentient life begins. Some posit that meaningful life begins at "viability" when a pre-born child is capable of surviving outside his mother's womb. This is problematic since technological advances continue to push back the time of viability to earlier and earlier ages.

On March 14, 2000, a tiny baby boy weighing only 14.3 ounces was born in Laguna Hills, California, at 24 weeks gestation.[3] An obstetrician who helped with the delivery called him the "pocket baby" because he could fit into the front pocket of the doctor's surgical scrubs. By June 10, the baby had grown to 3 1/2 pounds and was released from the

[1]New ultrasound technology developed by GE Medical Systems, http://www.gemedicalsystems.com/rad/us/4d/index.html.
[2]An Overview of Abortion in the U.S., the Alan Guttmacher Institute, www.agi-usa.org.
[3]*San Diego Union-Tribune,* June 12, 2000.

hospital. Only a few years ago, this baby, moments before birth, would have been considered "non-viable" and therefore not able to live, a conclusion his physician and his mother would find preposterous today.

It is easy to see how the "viability" standard does not make scientific sense; neither does it measure up to the standards of Biblical ethics. It flies in the face of Psalm 22:9-10, "But you are He that took me out of the womb; You made me trust while on my mother's breasts. I was cast upon You from birth. From my mother's womb You have been my God."

It is important to note that although some states have laws restricting abortion after "viability" they do not fully prevent these later-term abortions. Many elective abortions can legally take place at twenty-four weeks and later in several states, including California, New York, and Kansas.

Religious leaders from denominations that support abortion often claim that life does not begin until the child, like Adam, draws the first breath. They use Genesis 2:7 as their "proof text." This "first breath" theory also rejects basic biology. The pre-born child breathes in amniotic fluid and benefits from an exchange of gasses through the lungs, although he is still dependent on the oxygen that passes from the mother through the placental membranes into his blood. It also stands in opposition to other Bible verses such as Psalm 139:13-16:

> For you created my inmost being; you knit me
> together in my mother's womb. I praise you
> because I am fearfully and wonderfully made;
> your works are wonderful, I know that full well.
> My frame was not hidden from you when I was

made in the secret place. When I was woven together in the depths of the earth, your eyes saw my unformed body. All the days ordained for me were written in your book before one of them came to be.

The story of the incarnation of Christ is revealing as to when life begins. The angel told Mary in Luke 1:31, *"And behold, you will conceive in your womb and bring forth a Son, and shall call His name Jesus."* The angel explains how this will happen later in verse 35, *"The Holy Spirit will come upon you, and the power of the Highest will overshadow you; therefore, also, that Holy One who is to be born will be called the Son of God."* It is clearly at the point of fertilization, when Mary's egg joined with the power of the Holy Spirit, that the Word became flesh. At that moment, deity joined with humanity to produce the Savior who was fully God and fully man. Just as Jesus' life as a man began at fertilization in his mother's fallopian tube, so does all of ours.

God discusses the awareness of pre-born babies in Luke 1:41, *"And it happened, when Elizabeth heard the greeting of Mary, that the babe leaped in her womb; and Elizabeth was filled with the Holy Spirit."* John the Baptist, while still in his mother Elizabeth's womb, responded to the voice of Mary, who herself was pregnant with Jesus. The Greek word that is used in this verse to refer to John the Baptist is the same word used in Luke 2:16 to refer to the infant Christ child. In fact, John the Baptist enjoyed a special communion with God before birth as Luke 1:15 relates, *"He will also be filled with the Holy Spirit, even from his mother's womb."*

It is evident that Scripture values the lives of the born and pre-born equally. Exodus 21:18-24 is revealing. It prescribes punishment to anyone who would accidentally injure a pregnant woman and in so doing injure her pre-born baby. If the baby dies, it is required that the responsible party is executed, just as any other person guilty of murder. This places the lives of the pre-born on equal footing with those already born, without distinction as to gestational age, and classifies even the accidental taking of a pre-born child's life as murder. How much more then must God oppose the intentional destruction of human life made in His image at any stage of development? There can be no misunderstanding of Proverbs 6:17. God hates the hands that shed innocent blood.

In light of these verses, it is consistent with scripture as well as science, to accept that life begins at the moment of fertilization, when the father's sperm unites with the mother's egg and forms an entirely unique new living being, distinct from his or her parents. This baby, even at the earliest stage of development is made in God's image.

The Bible is clear as to why innocent people should not be killed. They bear the image of God. God told Noah in Genesis 9:5-6: *"Surely for your lifeblood I will demand a reckoning; . . . For in the image of God He made man."* We can now easily see that children in the womb are human beings, not potential humans, but real image-bearers of God, with all the protections granted to them by God through the Scriptures. These children are judicially innocent because they have not done anything but live inside mom, eat, and grow. Pre-born babies are incapable of committing, much less being found guilty, of any crime.

As human beings we have a unique distinction from all other creatures: we create our social environment. This environment is knit together by the laws, rules, customs and traditions that enable us to join together for mutual nurture, support and protection. When we pollute that social environment, we destroy the possibility of cherishing humanity as God's image-bearers – a pollution far more significant than any damage done to our external physical environment.

We have spoken of environmental pollution, but this is trivial when compared to what God must experience when He beholds pollution caused by shedding the innocent blood of babies through abortion. The putrid stench of innocent blood has defiled our nation. If, according to the Bible, the blood of just one innocent person is enough to contaminate the country and bring judgment, what will become of America where all fifty states are grossly polluted with the blood of many millions of innocent babies? It is this blood that cries out for justice.

In this chapter we have introduced the concept of *blood pollution*, this is, the spiritual filth that results from the taking of innocent human life. We have also established that unborn children are innocent human beings, and that the taking of their lives is murder, fully equivalent to the act of killing an innocent person after birth. We will now proceed to expose the complete depravity of abortion by summarizing how abortions are performed. This will help to establish the full bloodguiltiness that lies upon America. It will help us to understand God's perspective on the possible fate of our country in light of how He dealt with bloodguilty nations in biblical times.

Chapter 3

O LORD, you have searched me and you know me. You know when I sit and when I rise; you perceive my thoughts from afar. You discern my going out and my lying down; you are familiar with all my ways...For you created my inmost being; you knit me together in my mother's womb. I praise you because I am fearfully and wonderfully made; your works are wonderful, I know that full well. My frame was not hidden from you when I was made in the secret place. When I was woven together in the depths of the earth, your eyes saw my unformed body. All the days ordained for me were written in your book before one of them came to be.
Psalm 139:1-3 & 13-16

The Shedding of Blood

Abortions are performed in a number of ways. As we describe some of them, we will refrain from using emotionally charged language. It is not necessary. The clinical descriptions of abortion are enough to evoke emotion without the aid of rhetoric.

Approximately ninety percent of all abortions are performed between six and twelve weeks gestation.[1] The usual method uses a suction machine that develops a powerful vacuum. A tube from the machine is pushed through

---

[1] An Overview of Abortion in the U.S., the Alan Guttmacher Institute, www.agi-usa.org. [88.1% of abortions take place in first trimester.]

the cervix, and fragment by fragment the baby is violently sucked into a jar where a screen will separate blood from flesh. The killing is completed by severing the placenta from the uterus and scraping clean the uterine wall. The abortionist, by law, must visually identify the body parts within the strainer. He must determine if he has removed the entire body. Any tissue that is left behind, such as arms, legs, hands, torso, or skull, will cause a serious, possibly life-threatening, infection for the mother. Once that determination has been made, the murder has been completed with far more skill and training than displayed by your average, hired assassin. The entire abortion procedure usually takes less than ten minutes.

During the second thirteen weeks of pregnancy, the child grows rapidly and his tiny bones begin to calcify. At this stage the baby is far too large to be sucked through a tube. The abortion method of choice at this stage of development is called Dilatation and Evacuation, or D&E.

In order to prevent tearing the mother's cervix during the D&E, the abortionist must gradually enlarge the cervix, the opening mouth of the uterus, with "laminaria." These are tightly wound sticks of seaweed about the thickness of a pencil lead that are inserted into the cervix and left for a day or more. As the laminaria absorbs the mother's natural body fluids, the seaweed expands, slowly forcing open the cervix. The abortionist now has a dilated opening through which he can insert a tong-like instrument that he uses to grasp and tear apart the living baby. First an arm is grasped: rotate, pull hard, and off it comes. He tosses it in the pan. Perhaps then may come a leg. He rotates and pulls but the muscles and tendons tend to be a bit harder to tear off. After a little more wrenching, it yields. Soon, the baby is dead, violently torn limb from limb without a drop of anesthesia. If someone did this to a dog in front of an abortion clinic to make a point, there would be laws on the books that would put him in jail for a long time. But it is not a dog we have just described, and there are no laws to come to the aid of the children about to be dismembered in the abortion clinics across our nation.

However, the abortionist is not finished yet. The dead baby's head and torso still remain trapped within the uterus. The cervix opening is still too small in diameter to accommodate their size. With his tongs, he searches blindly until finally the skull is caught in the crushing grip of his "Cranialclast,"[2] whose name translated from the Latin is literally "skull-crusher." The skull collapses under the force, spilling its gray contents as it passes through the cervical opening. He is almost finished now. The abortionist completes his contracted killing with a spoon-shaped knife called a curette. With this he scrapes and scoops until at last he is sure he has removed all the tissue and bone fragments.

In many cases, the bloody pieces of the baby will be dumped into a bucket, not unlike one of those cheap ice cream buckets one can purchase at the grocery store, and sent to a pathology lab[3] where the tissues will be briefly weighed and examined. If all the body parts are accounted for, the remains are shipped off with the rest of the medical waste for incineration. Depending on the clinic, the remains may be put through a meat grinder then flushed down the drain, or run through an industrial sized garbage disposal. Still others may be tossed into the dumpster with the rest of the day's

---

[2] A description and illustration can be found in the Online Catalog of REDA Instruments, Singapore, http://www.reda.com.sg/scripts/browse/Catalog2.asp?pcat = 54&pcatname = OBSTETRICS
[3] Photographic evidence was taken at a pathology lab in Los Angeles, California, by Tim Wilson in 2000, and can be viewed at www.operationrescue.org.

trash, creating a serious public health hazard. It has been reported that playing children have discovered improperly disposed of aborted babies on more than one occasion. [4]

Although some states have attempted to strictly regulate abortions after viability, other states allow abortion for almost any reason through the ninth month of pregnancy. Usually, loopholes can easily be found around late-term abortion restrictions, allowing the clever abortionist to ply his trade with little inconvenience. In the weeks just prior to birth, a number of methods are employed to terminate the baby's life.

Using ultrasound imaging, the abortionist locates the tiny, beating heart through the mother's swollen tummy. He then inserts a long needle through the mother's abdomen, injecting the baby's heart with a drug that paralyzes the tiny muscle. Labor is then induced using prostaglandin, a drug that causes the uterus to contract violently. The mother then delivers an intact but dead late-term baby.

Prostaglandin is sometimes used alone to expel the child through the induction of premature labor, although this is now somewhat rare because of the high risk of what are called in the industry, "complications." Prostaglandin causes rapid and powerful contractions as well as severe nausea, vomiting, and diarrhea. In fact, the contractions can be so violent that women's uteruses have been known to rupture

---

[4] *The Milwaukee Sentinel*, May 14, 1984. This story reported that police arrested four children ages 4-11, who were throwing a fetus off a bridge. The youngsters had retrieved 22 aborted babies from a nearby dumpster. When asked what they were doing, the children replied that they were playing with "little people."
"54 Babies" by George F. Will, *The Washington Post*, December 3, 1998.

and babies decapitated in the process of delivery. It is also not unusual for a child to be expelled from the womb while still alive, a complication most dreaded by late term abortionists. A live birth during an abortion creates a plethora of ethical dilemmas for the healer-turned-killer. Since the intent of the mother was to take the life of her child, should the doctor simply kill the baby outside the womb? Should he be manually strangled or simply left to die in his own afterbirth? This is very stressful on the medical staff because they are brought face to face with the reality of what they do to earn their wages.[5] It is easy to see why few abortionists use this technique any more.

Another method, hysterotomy, is abortion by cesarean section. It is generally used only when other late-term methods fail or if life-threatening complications for the mother develop. The womb is opened surgically and the child is then killed by the doctor *mano a mano*.

Currently, the most common and probably best-known method of aborting late term babies is Dilatation and Extraction, or D&X. This procedure is popularly known as the "Partial-Birth Abortion." After adequately dilating the cervix, the abortionist uses forceps to reach into the birth canal to grasp the leg of the fully developed five-to-nine month old baby. He forcefully wrenches the child, feet first, from the safe home inside the mother until only the head is left inside the birth canal. By now the baby is kicking and struggling for life. Next, the "doctor" pierces the skull and vacuums the brain from the tiny head. The abortionist then

[5]The Born Alive Infants Protection Act of 2001 was written specifically for the protection of babies born alive during an attempted abortion. The text may be found at the Catalog of Congressional Bills web site under the 107th Congress, House Bills, (HR): http:/www.access.gpo.gov/congress/billsindex.html.

collapses the baby's skull to remove the now lifeless child.

Abortionists find certain advantages to this method. First, the chances of a live baby emerging from the birth canal are dramatically reduced. One abortionist interviewed on a nationally broadcast radio program admitted that a second benefit to the breech delivery of the Partial-Birth Abortion is the fact that one cannot hear the baby screaming as his skull is pierced and emptied.[6] Thirdly, the abortionist may be able to make extra money from offering the parents additional services, such as a memorial ceremony for their dead child, complete with baptism, if desired, and an urn for the ashes if cremation is requested.

The fourth benefit of the D&X procedure is least discussed by the abortionists. It involves the prospect of being able to sell the undamaged organs to biotech labs and pharmaceutical companies for research – including ovaries and eggs, which are harvested for future experiments or infertile couples.[7] According to a price list obtained from Open Lines, a pathology business in West Frankfort, Illinois, brains of aborted babies are especially valuable. Laboratories purchase the fetal brains from abortion clinics then use them to develop experimental treatments for people with nervous disorders like Parkinson's Disease. (Treatments developed from such tissue have thus far proved to be unsuccessful, and in some cases, disastrous to the human subjects on which they were tested.[8]) Thus with very little extra effort on their part, the abortionists add to their large fees for late-term

[6]This information was related to the author by Rev. Joseph Foreman, who personally heard the remarks.
[7]"Transplantation of Aborted Fetal Eggs (Ovum): A Short Analysis" by Lawrence F. Roberge, M. S., 1994.
[8]AP, MSNBC, "Fetal cell transplant fails to cure Parkinson's" March 7, 2001.

abortions the cash from the thriving body parts market. Meanwhile, the mother gets nothing for her trouble but an empty womb, drained pocketbook, and perhaps a memorial service for the child she paid to have killed.[9]

It is important to realize that the acts of killing described in this chapter happen every day behind the closed doors of abortion clinics with euphemistic names like "Planned Parenthood," "Family Planning Associates," "Woman Care," "Women's Medical Clinic," and "Pregnancy Control Clinic." The blood of the babies who die there runs red just like yours. Their arms and legs look like yours. They feel pain just like you do. Their body parts function and are harvested just like yours could be. They are human beings created in the likeness and image of God Almighty, just like you.

After considering the humanity of the pre-born children and the brutal means by which abortion takes their lives, several questions arise. Does the termination of these lives matter to God? If so, why? If God does see their blood as they are torn apart or their heads are crushed, what will He do about it? As the voice of their shed blood speaks from the ground for vengeance, how will God respond? Does He care that we permit this shedding of blood even when we are not doing it ourselves or encouraging others to do it?

If the Scriptures show that God does care about the lives of the pre-born and considers abortion to be murder, as we intend to show, then this crime is greater than we can possibly imagine. It is an attack against God, a Declaration of

---

[9]Recommending reading: *Bioethics in an Age of Emerging Biotechnology: A Christian Response to Human Embryo Experimentation* by Cheryl Sullenger, Restoration Press, 2001.

War against the very Creator of the Universe. It is an assault against the created order and against civilization itself. One can see why people react with intensity when it is brought to light in even a casual conversation or incidentally in a sermon.

To understand God's viewpoint in the taking of pre-born human life, it is necessary to look more closely at the questions of **guilt** and **innocence**. What does the Bible have to say about these important terms, and how do they impact the matter of bloodguilt in our nation? The next chapter addresses these key questions.

Chapter 4

*"**W**hy do you bring charges against me? You have all rebelled against me," declares the LORD. "In vain I punished your people; they did not respond to correction. Your sword has devoured your prophets like a ravening lion." You of this generation, consider the word of the LORD: "Have I been a desert to Israel or a land of great darkness? Why do my people say, `We are free to roam; we will come to you no more'? Does a maiden forget her jewelry, a bride her wedding ornaments? Yet my people have forgotten me, days without number. How skilled you are at pursuing love! Even the worst of women can learn from your ways.* **On your clothes men find the lifeblood of the innocent poor,** *though you did not catch them breaking in.* **Yet in spite of all this you say, `I am innocent; he is not angry with me.'** *But I will pass judgment on you because you say, `I have not sinned.'"*
Jeremiah 2:29-35

Innocence

Jesus Christ was beaten and hung naked on a Roman cross. He was dying. The inhabitants of Jerusalem hurried past the three crosses, glancing up only long enough to read the unusual inscription on a piece of parchment nailed above Christ's head. "This is Jesus the King of the Jews," it read in three different languages. Some must have briefly stopped to wonder at this attribution, only to shrug it off as merely another matter of political intrigue and hurry on about their day's business thinking it best not to question the Roman brand of justice.

Jesus died the death of a common criminal, crucified between two thieves. His hands and feet were pierced with iron nails. Jesus' head was crowned with thorns; His body was whipped and beaten. It was an excruciating, humiliating, and agonizing death.

The indignity was compounded by the fact that Jesus was innocent. His mock trial before the Sanhedrin was based upon a lie. It was an act of injustice provoked by jealousy and a sense of self-preservation of the power hungry Jewish leaders. Jesus was then taken before Pilate where He was falsely accused, but never legally convicted, of the crime of subversion (Luke 23:2), yet He was paying for the "crime" with His life. In contrast, the men who were crucified on the left and right of Jesus had been justly convicted of their crimes and sentenced to death. One of these criminals even admitted, as he was dying, that they had rightly earned the death penalty. In rebuking his companion, who blasphemed Jesus, one of the criminals said, *"Don't you fear God, since you are under the same sentence? We are punished justly, for we are getting what our deeds deserve. But this man has done nothing wrong"* (Luke 23:40-41).

The Roman government alone had the authority to execute criminals within its jurisdiction. Once the two thieves were found guilty of capital crimes, the Romans had every right to nail them to a cross. But Jesus was another matter and the Roman governor of Palestine knew it.

The night before Christ's trial, the wife of Governor Pontius Pilate had been stirred by troubling dreams of Jesus.

She sent an urgent message to her husband begging him to have nothing to do with Christ's death, for she believed Jesus was innocent. Prompted by her pleadings, Pilate offered a compromise. As was the custom, Pilate had intended to release a prisoner of the people's choosing during the Passover celebration. In an attempt to extricate himself from the delicate situation with the Jews, he offered to release Jesus. However, the Jewish religious leaders had already convinced the crowd to ask for the release of Barabbas, a man found guilty of insurrection and murder, (Mark 15:7). As Pilate urged the Jews to ask for the release of Jesus, the crowd became unruly, chanting for the crucifixion of Christ. Pontius Pilate succumbed to the desires of the boisterous Jewish mob. He let Barabbas go free. Convinced though he was of the innocence of Christ, Pilate sent Jesus off to His death. He attempted in vain to absolve himself of the bloodguilt as he washed his hands and falsely declared, *"I am innocent of this man's blood. It is your responsibility!"* (Matthew 27:24).

Jesus had not broken a single civil law, was never lawfully convicted of any crime, nor had He committed any sin before God. Jesus was both judicially innocent before men and spiritually innocent before God. Jesus was the only man to ever achieve a truly innocent life. The blood that flowed from Christ's beaten body was the blood of an innocent man. Not only had the Romans shed the innocent blood of Jesus, but they had allowed a legally convicted, violent, and murderous man be pardoned and released. The Romans had perverted justice.

In order to understand the forms of guilt and innocence we must first understand the authority structure, or Law Order, under which God ordained for man to live. In His infinite wisdom, God created a set of laws that mankind must follow in order to experience the blessings He has for us in this life. Since He is the ultimate Judge and King, our obedience to His Legal Order is obligatory. Although God Himself retains ultimate authority over His Creation, He has delegated some of His authority to man by ordaining the four forms of government here on Earth. Because God is a God of proper order, (2 Samuel 23:5), these four structures of authority are intended to guide mankind through daily life.

1. Personal or self government (2 Timothy 2:15)
2. Family government (Genesis 3:16)
3. Civil government (Romans 13:1)
4. Church government (Acts 16:4-5)

Although God created life and He alone has the authority to determine when life can be taken away (Job 1:21), He has given authority to the civil government to take a human life on His behalf when administering judgment to the criminally guilty in capital offenses.

> *For rulers hold no terror for those who do right, but for those who do wrong. Do you want to be free from fear of the one in authority? Then do what is right and he will commend you. For he is God's servant to do you good. But if you do wrong, be afraid,* **for he does not bear the sword for nothing.** *He is God's servant, an agent of wrath to bring punishment on the wrongdoer* (Romans 13: 3-4).

The civil government alone, of all earthly institutions, has the God-given power of the sword, to take the life of the judicially guilty without incurring bloodguilt. The individual under the auspices of self-government does not have this authority nor has it been delegated to the family or to the local church. However, this power is not *carte blanche*. The power of the state to execute the guilty is regulated by God's legal order. Morally, it can only take a guilty human life for specific capital offenses and then only through due process. Kidnappers, murderers, rapists, violent criminals, and traitors, to name just a few, have all been put to death under the power of the state and with the approval of God.

Judicial guilt should not be confused with spiritual guilt. We are not discussing the issue of original sin and how that makes all men guilty, spiritually, before God. We are talking about acts that people have done or not done themselves. Scripture confirms that human beings, the pre-born included, have the right to have their lives protected as long as they have not themselves committed a crime worthy of death. In fact, the pre-born child is incapable of committing such a crime. Paul commented upon this innocence as he discussed Jacob and his twin brother Esau while they still resided within Rebecca's womb, *"before the twins were born or had done anything good or bad..."* (Romans 9:11). In that respect the child in the womb is the paradigm of judicial innocence. That is, he or she has done nothing for which he could be convicted in a criminal court.

"Innocent blood" and "murder" are interchangeable concepts. Murder is the unjust or unlawful killing of an innocent person. The word "murder" is never used in conjunction with the execution of the guilty or wicked. That is why translations as radically different as the New International and the New King James Versions of the Bible, among others, translate the Sixth Commandment in Exodus 20:13, *"You shall not murder."* This commandment pertains only to **innocent** human life that is wrongfully taken. It is God's foundation for everything else He says about murder including, *"You shall not shed innocent blood."* Therefore, the execution of murderers found guilty under the law is not a violation of the Sixth Commandment, but rather an enforcement of it.

Biblically speaking, how far can a government go in putting its citizens to death for their crimes? Many of us have pled guilty to one or more traffic violations, making us guilty of an infraction or misdemeanor. More seriously, what about the embezzler who bilked his company out of a hundred thousand dollars? The former president of the United States, Bill Clinton, received a severe reprimand from the State of Arkansas for his misdeeds and later confessed to lying under oath. Can one be sentenced to death for these crimes? No. The penalty must fit the crime. It can be seen from the following verses that crimes against someone's property or even one's person required restitution, but a crime against his life was different. Murder was always a capital offense.

> *If anyone takes the life of a human being, he must be put to death. Anyone who takes the life of someone's animal must make restitution – life for life. If anyone injures his neighbor, whatever he has done must be done to him: fracture for fracture, eye for eye, tooth for tooth. As he has injured the other, so he is to be injured. Whoever kills an animal must make restitution, but whoever kills a man must be put to death* (Leviticus 24:17-21).

There are, however, people who make up the vast majority of the population who have not been convicted of a crime. By and large every person not behind bars today is to be considered innocent, legally speaking, until proven guilty in a court of law. Their lawful innocence begins at the time of their conception and continues through natural death unless they are convicted of a crime through due process. These people could also be called legally blameless. One of the rightful duties of government is to provide for the protection of the blameless. It is a terrible injustice for the innocent to die unjustly, and for the shedding of innocent blood to go unpunished.

A society is often critiqued by how it treats the most innocent or helpless individuals living within its jurisdiction. Women and children are generally considered to be the weakest physically, among mankind. Honorable people will always strive to safeguard them and keep them out of harm's way. The elderly and infirm may come next on the list of people needing special assistance. The Bible points out that widows, orphans, the sick, and the needy require particular care, (Proverbs 31:8, James 1:27, Matthew 25:31-46). It is a command of God to protect, guard, defend and look after human life – God's image-bearers.

Yet, legally blameless people, fashioned in the image and likeness of the Creator, are brutally murdered every day. The babies dying in abortion clinics and hospitals are given no trial; they have no judge, no jury, and no right of appeal. Instead, they face the murderous executioners who are paid to administer gross injustice upon these weak and vulnerable human beings. The blood of pre-born babies is being spilled in every state, in every major city across our nation. This innocent blood cries out for justice.

> *Son of man, say to the land, "You are a land that has had no rain or showers in the day of wrath." **There is a conspiracy of her princes within her like a roaring lion tearing its prey;** they devour people, take treasures and*

precious things and make many widows within her. **Her priests do violence to my law and profane my holy things;** *they do not distinguish between the holy and the common; they teach that there is no difference between the unclean and the clean; and they shut their eyes to the keeping of my Sabbaths, so that I am profaned among them.* **Her officials within her are like wolves tearing their prey; they shed blood and kill people to make unjust gain.** *Her prophets whitewash these deeds for them by false visions and lying divinations. They say, "This is what the Sovereign LORD says"—when the LORD has not spoken. The people of the land practice extortion and commit robbery; they oppress the poor and needy and mistreat the alien, denying them justice.*

I looked for a man among them who would build up the wall and stand before me in the gap on behalf of the land so I would not have to destroy it, but I found none. So I will pour out my wrath on them and consume them with my fiery anger, bringing down on their own heads all they have done, declares the Sovereign LORD (Ezekiel 22:24-31).

Observing what is happening in our nation to the innocent pre-born compared with God's laws and rules and judgments, a profoundly serious discrepancy can be seen. The Lord is looking for those who will do justice where there is gross injustice. Those who love mercy and justice, God's people, must step up – and soon – to protect the innocent or God's judgment will descend upon our land.

Chapter 5

*This is what the LORD says: Do what is just and right.
Rescue from the hand of his oppressor the one who has
been robbed. Do no wrong or violence to the alien,
the fatherless or the widow, and do not shed
innocent blood in this place.*

Jeremiah 22:3

The Voice of Innocent Blood

Cain and Abel were conversing in a field when
Cain rose up in anger and struck down his brother Abel. Abel
was legally innocent when his life's blood flowed from his
body into the ground. God spent very few words recounting
the details of that violent act in Genesis 4:8, but the trail of
blood beginning there runs through the entire Word of God.
This was the first murder – the first innocent human blood
shed on Earth.

Afterward, God spoke with Cain, who refused to own
up to his brother's killing. Genesis 4:10-11 makes a startling
disclosure:

> The LORD said, "What have you done? Listen!
> Your brother's blood cries out to me from the
> ground. Now you are under a curse and driven
> from the ground which opened its mouth to
> receive your brother's blood from your hand."

There are two noteworthy points here. First, the innocent blood of Abel had a voice. It cried out to God as a testimony against Cain for justice. Why would blood have such a powerful voice? Leviticus 17:11 teaches, *"For the life of a creature is in the blood."* Without blood, the creatures of the earth, including man, could not exist. It is the blood that carries the life-sustaining oxygen and nutrients to every cell of the body, then carries away the waste products so that the organism can properly grow and thrive. The spilling of blood represents, very literally, the spilling forth of life. When the blood that is shed belongs to an innocent person, it bears witness before God to injustice and murder in a similar way that an eyewitness might testify about a crime in court. In fact, with the advent of DNA testing, blood evidence is being used as important testimony to convict murderers even though there may be no human witness to the crime. The blood, in these cases, speaks volumes.

The second point seen in Genesis 4:10-11 is the consequence of having shed innocent blood. The murderer comes under a curse from God. This is the curse of bloodguilt. Bloodguilt brings upon men, communities, and nations very real and devastating consequences, which will be discussed later.

Of all sins, God particularly abhors murder. He places the highest value on human life because that life alone, in all of His creation, was fashioned in His own image (Genesis 1:27). Although the entire creation cries out for a Redeemer (Romans 8:19-22), it is mankind upon whom God has placed His heart. Because of His desire to redeem His fallen image-bearers, God sent His only Son to earth. Jesus came that we might not perish but have eternal life (John 3:16). God did not love us in a general way, or as mankind, in some vague sense (Ephesians 1). Rather, He says that He sought out each sheep personally (Matthew 18:12ff). He writes each name on the palms of his hand (Isaiah 49:16). He knows his sheep by name (John 10:3). He gives to those who overcome, a stone with a new name written on it known only to them and God (Revelation 2:17).

The fact that God loved mankind enough to send His own Son to suffer and die should be reason enough to believe that God has a high regard for the life of each person – even those who are not redeemed but will gain the benefit of living among those who are.

A high value for human life can be found today reflected in secular civil law. Legislation is continually being passed to ensure that innocent blood is not spilled. There are laws that require motorists to stop at marked intersections in order to prevent the shedding of innocent blood. There are laws that require certain products to meet a variety of safety standards to ensure that innocent people are not accidentally injured or killed. Although legislators often run amok with volumes of unbiblical rules and regulations, many of the laws related to safety reflect a Biblical respect for human life by providing for its protection. Murder is one of the highest crimes a person can commit in the United States and is one of the few crimes that still warrants the death penalty.

The murder of any of God's image-bearers is an assault on God Himself. When one man murders another, he is doing violence to the image of God reflected in man. Furthermore, the murderer usurps God's authority and the authority God has given to the civil government by wielding the power of life and death in his own hand. That power and authority over life belongs to God alone and to those upon whom He grants it (Romans 13:1).

The shedding of innocent blood is so abhorrent to God that He reserves His divine hatred for the hands that shed it (Proverbs 6:17). He will require an accounting for every murdered human being. *"And for your lifeblood I will surely demand an accounting. I will demand an accounting from every animal. And from each man, too, I will demand an accounting for the life of his fellow man"* (Genesis 9:5). In the very next verse God decrees the death penalty for anyone who sheds the blood of an innocent person. *"Whoever sheds the blood of man, by man shall his blood be shed; for in the image of God has God made man."*

This brings us back to the first murderer, Cain. If justice demands that the life of the murderer be forfeited, why was Cain allowed to live? For the answer, we must again consider the forms of government instituted by God. At this point, only one family existed. Later, as man obeyed the dominion mandate and began to multiply, civil governments were required to maintain peace and safety for the inhabitants of a particular area. It is not given to the family, according to the Law Order of God, to execute criminals. Rousas J. Rushdoony's remarks on this subject are enlightening:

> Family discipline can mean disinheritance; it can mean denouncing a child to the civil authorities. But the death penalty is reserved to God and the state. To give that power to the family is to destroy the inner tie that binds the family. The protection of Cain was thus not with reference to Cain as a person but the life of the family and its law sphere. (Institutes of Biblical Law, Vol. 1, 1973, page 361.)

Since civil government now exists, we cannot look to the exception of Cain as a reason to excuse murderers from justice. The fact that Cain was cursed by God and put out of the family shows respect and protection for the life that God created and the order He expects to govern it.

We have seen that when Cain murdered Abel, the voice of Abel's blood cried out to God from the ground (Genesis 4:10). However this is not the only example of the voice of innocent blood. Revelation 6:9-10 speaks of those martyred for the faith crying out from under the altar in heaven for Christ to avenge their blood. The voice of innocent blood demands justice for injustice. It cries for vengeance and retribution – a curse.

When innocent blood speaks, God listens. The blood of murdered people will always cry out to God for vengeance until their murderers are properly held accountable or when the day of final justice comes upon all mankind. It is a sobering thought to consider that God hears their cries and guarantees that He will exact judgment. Since murder is an attack on God's image and authority, one can be sure that His vengeance, when it comes, will be inescapable.

> *"If I whet My glittering sword, and My hand takes hold on judgment, I will render vengeance to My enemies, and repay those who hate Me"* (Deuteronomy 32:41 NKJV).

Stop for a moment and think of all the murdered people from Abel until today. God is listening to the cry of all the people whose lives have been cut short by the hand of a fellowman where justice was not properly meted out. God sees all the murder and bloodshed even when it is done in secret. From the hidden murder of a nameless, homeless man in a lonely, filthy alley to the death of John F. Kennedy, assassinated in a Dallas, Texas, motorcade before the whole world, God sees. God hears.

There is also a segment of mankind murdered in darkness, forgotten and unseen. These are the pre-born children who die every day. These aborted children are of equal value in the eyes of God to you and me, yet they are neglected daily. Their bodies are dismembered behind the shroud of the abortion clinic doors and discarded as medical waste. To us, but not God, all of them are nameless, faceless babies who will never see the light of day nor take even one breath of fresh air. They die alone, unwanted, and unloved. Their only crime was the inconvenience of their conception. Second only to Christ, they are the most innocent among our human race. Unlike all other men, no outward sin has ever been committed by them.

The innocent blood of aborted babies has a message for those who claim the name of Christ. It stands as a testimony of conviction against the Church for her inaction, allowing the murder of so many. The voice of innocent blood cries out to Christians for help and protection, but so few seem to hear or even care.

Daily, the babies' blood cries out to God for justice and for vengeance. Their blood speaks to Him of the injustice of their untimely deaths, regret for the lives that will never be lived, and of revenge for the families they will never produce or enjoy. God will heed the voice of their innocent blood. His hand is reaching toward the hilt of His glittering sword and He will aim the vengeful stroke of justice upon the necks of those who stood by just as much as upon those responsible for the slaughter.

The abortion clinics, euphemistically called "women's reproductive health centers," where millions of innocent children have succumbed to the abortionist's knife, enjoy an air of respectability in communities across our country. One can hardly distinguish them from the other, more reputable businesses that line the streets of our cities and towns. But under that thin facade of respectability and normalcy lurks a bizarre and largely unknown world of murder, greed, power struggles, and perversion.

Chapter 6

For they have forsaken me and made this a place of foreign gods; they have burned sacrifices in it to gods that neither they nor their fathers nor the kings of Judah ever knew, and they have filled this place with the blood of the innocent. They have built the high places of Baal to burn their sons in the fire as offerings to Baal – something I did not command or mention, nor did it enter my mind. So beware, the days are coming, declares the LORD, when people will no longer call this place Topheth or the Valley of Ben Hinnom, but the Valley of Slaughter.
Jeremiah 19:4-6

The Bloodshed Fills the Streets

Nestled in the heartland of America is the quaint city of Wichita, Kansas. Wichita is geographically near the center of the United States of America. The small town, by American standards, is quickly growing into an economic hub for the heartland. Home to aviation giants like Cessna and Boeing, and the great American camping icon, Coleman, not to mention Pizza Hut, the city of 300,000 people quietly exists in near utopia.

Driving on the two-lane roads that extend for miles through the vast wheat fields of Kansas one can almost hear the poet sing, "Oh, beautiful for spacious skies for amber waves of grain." The American plains are beautiful and the folks are down home, salt-of-the-earth types of people. Yet this almost idyllic community embodies an overwhelming irony. Here is a true account of a group of British tourists.

After traveling a thousand nautical miles to reach North America, a family of English travelers rented a big American car and set out to see the sights. However, they did not have the typical Midwestern tourist sites on their agenda. Instead, the Brits detoured to Wichita in the late spring of 2001.

What these vacationers desired to see was a sight whose reputation has traveled far outside the boxy borders of the Sunflower State. The attraction they sought is known to desperate women worldwide as a safe haven for those in need of very special services. On East Kellogg Avenue, situated between two new car dealerships, is a state-of-the-art medical facility of international reputation. Women travel from around the world to Wichita and stay in the fancy La Quinta Hotel to undergo a two or three-day medical procedure.

The tourists mentioned here took time out of their holiday to visit the world-renowned Women's Health Care Services owned by Dr. George Tiller. They were aware that many of their own countrywomen travel here to get his expert care. The British Broadcasting Corporation regularly enlightens viewers on the advanced medical attention one can find only across the Atlantic.

Now, Dr. George Tiller is no ordinary man and his Women's Health Care Services is an extraordinary facility. Tiller's credentials are extensive and quite impressive. His specialty is narrowly focused and his skills are so unusual that few in the medical world claim to be his peer.

George Tiller is an abortionist and his medical facility is an abortion mill. Tiller will kill any child, at any age, at least as long as the child's head is still inside the mother's body. Late term abortions are his specialty. So few doctors are willing to perform abortions on the larger babies that Tiller is able to demand a handsome price for his work. His fees can reach $10,000 or more.[1] George Tiller executes babies from close to the moment of conception to healthy, full-term babies in the ninth month of pregnancy. Tiller is good at what he does; so good that during the 1990s the abortion rate in Kansas increased thirty percent due to Tiller's salesmanship.[2] He has turned the amber wheat fields of Kansas into his own personal killing fields, as it were, staining them scarlet with the innocent blood of pre-born babies.

While record numbers of abortion clinics across America were closing due to pro-life opposition, George Tiller was accelerating his business and expanding his facility.[3] Tiller actually purchased the two abutting properties and tripled the size of his abortion mill. His clinic looks more like a warehouse for top-secret technologies than a medical office. There are no exterior windows. The complex is completely fenced with video cameras scanning the perimeter while an armed security guard greets every customer.

An incinerator's smokestack protrudes above the mill's flat roof, looming over Wichita's busy Kellogg Avenue. The full-sized, industrial-capacity human crematorium is

---

[1]This figure is a conservative estimate based on conversations with an anonymous employee of Tiller's. His fees could very well be three to four time that figure depending on insurance payouts for very late abortions for fetal abnormality.
[2]Kansas Department of Health and Environment web site: http://www.kdhe.state.ks.us/hci/as01/as2001.html.
[3]http://www.drtiller.com/facil.html.

normally found only in mortuaries, but Tiller needs this one to dispose of the grisly remains of his state-of-the-art medical killing center. Here one can observe and taste the putrid smoke of burning human flesh billowing from the 10,000 square foot abortuary.

Ever looking for new ways to increase his profit margin, the enterprising Tiller not only incinerates the bodies of the babies he has killed, but sells their ashes back to parents in a keepsake urn.[4] As a proud member of Reformation Lutheran Church in Wichita, Tiller actually calls in clergy members to his abortion mill to provide memorial services and baptisms for the babies that he aborts, if the parents so desire.[5] It is ironic that Tiller's killing business could not thrive without this church's consent, support, and protection. Admittedly this is a ghoulish picture, all the more so because it bears striking similarities to the Nazis' Final Solution. Though the method of selection is different, the purpose and result is similar: Tiller, like Hitler, desires to cleanse the gene pool of unwanted people and help free those who are burdened with the care of unnecessary, unwanted and unloved lives. And like Hitler, Tiller incinerates his victims with the acquiescence of the church.

Regretfully, the British tourists could not seem to make the obvious connection between Women's Health Services and Hitler's Dachau and Auschwitz. They could not see the similarity between Joseph Mengele and George Tiller – twin "innovative" doctors of their ages.

God speaks of similar atrocities committed by man with disturbing regularity throughout the Bible. These verses

[4]http://www.drtiller.com/remembrance.html.
[5]http://www.drtiller.com/chap.html.

read today as if they could have been written about America's modern atrocity, the abortion holocaust. The corollary is inescapable. Again and again throughout the Scriptures, we can see how God recounts the horror of innocent bloodshed and how it soon becomes a plague to the nation it defiles. Quite aside from any threatened future judgment God might bring, bloodshed itself brings its own intrinsic curse. Witness the agonized response of mothers, brothers, fathers, grandparents and even bystanders who become terribly upset at any reminder of their past involvement in child killing.

Bloodshed fills the streets now as it did during the Biblical eras of rebellion. Read the following verses and consider if America is any better than the Israel of antiquity, which God devastated because of their wanton disregard for human life. Can any nation be exempt from the judgment of God that comes on those who pollute their land with innocent blood?

> *Jeremiah 19:4-6 For they have forsaken me and made this a place of foreign gods; they have burned sacrifices in it to gods that neither they nor their fathers nor the kings of Judah ever knew, and **they have filled this place with the blood of the innocent**. They have built the high places of Baal to burn their sons in the fire as offerings to Baal – something I did not command or mention, nor did it enter my mind. **So beware, the days are coming, declares the LORD, when people will no longer call this place Topheth or the Valley of Ben Hinnom, but the Valley of Slaughter.***

Tophet was a site in Northern Israel where human sacrifice, particularly that of children, took place to the

Phoenician idols of Baal and Ashtoreth. The word "tophet" has come to mean any depository of human remains. One remarkable tophet found amid the ruins of ancient Carthage, has recently yielded evidence that pre-born children were purposely aborted to be offered as sacrifices to the adopted idols of the Phoenicians, who imported their murderous idolatry to that busy sea port.[6] Our nation's abortion mills are little different than the ancient valley of Tophet where innocent children were sacrificed. The comparison to George Tiller's Wichita abortion center, complete with crematorium, is unmistakable.

> **2 Kings 21:16 Moreover, Manasseh also shed so much innocent blood that he filled Jerusalem from end to end** – besides the sin that he had caused Judah to commit, so that they did evil in the eyes of the LORD.

> **Psalm 79:1-3** O God, the nations have invaded your inheritance; they have defiled your holy temple, they have reduced Jerusalem to rubble. They have given the dead bodies of your servants as food to the birds of the air, the flesh of your saints to the beasts of the earth. **They have poured out blood like water all around Jerusalem, and there is no one to bury the dead.**

> **Hosea 6:8** Gilead is a city of wicked men, **stained with footprints of blood.**

> **Joel 3:19** But Egypt will be desolate, Edom a

---

[6]"Sacrifices," a one-hour episode that aired on the Discovery Channel's "Discover Magazine" in October, 2002.

desert waste, because of **violence done to the people of Judah, in whose land they shed innocent blood.**

Habakkuk 2:8 Because you have plundered many nations, **the peoples who are left will plunder you. For you have shed man's blood**; you have destroyed lands and cities and everyone in them.

Ezekiel 9:9-10 He answered me, "The sin of the house of Israel and Judah is exceedingly great; **the land is full of bloodshed and the city is full of injustice**. They say, `The LORD has forsaken the land; the LORD does not see.' So I will not look on them with pity or spare them, but I will bring down on their own heads what they have done.**"

Ezekiel 7:23 Prepare chains, because the **land is full of bloodshed** and the city is full of violence.

The shedding of innocent blood was the sin responsible for the enslavement and captivity of apostate Israel and Judah as well as the devastation of a number of communities and nations. In like manner, America is full of the blood of millions of pre-born children. Does enslavement await our nation as well?

Psalms 106:34-42 They did not destroy the peoples as the LORD had commanded them, but they mingled with the nations and adopted their customs. They worshiped their idols, which became a snare to them. **They**

sacrificed their sons and their daughters to demons. They shed innocent blood, the blood of their sons and daughters, whom they sacrificed to the idols of Canaan, and the land was desecrated by their blood. They defiled themselves by what they did; by their deeds they prostituted themselves. Therefore the LORD was angry with his people and abhorred his inheritance. He handed them over to the nations, and their foes ruled over them. Their enemies oppressed them and subjected them to their power.

Ezekiel 36:18 So I poured out my wrath on them because they had shed blood in the land and because they had defiled it with their idols.

Innocent bloodshed brought a curse upon the once promised land once "flowing with milk and honey." If God reacts to the killing today as He did then, America is jeopardizing her very existence by allowing abortion to continue.

Jeremiah 2:34 ...you have also taught the wicked women your ways. Also on your skirts is found the blood of the lives of the poor innocents. I have not found it by secret search, but plainly on all these things. (NKJV)

It is almost as though the people of Judah were either unaware or in denial that the blood of their murder victims cried out to God in testimony against them. America today believes she is a righteous nation of freedom and justice that God must bless because her people deserve it. How like Judah in attitude we are today! Will we also share her fate?

> **Ezekiel 16:36-38** *This is what the Sovereign LORD says: Because you poured out your wealth and exposed your nakedness in your promiscuity with your lovers, and because of all your detestable idols,* **and because you gave them your children's blood**, *therefore I am going to gather all your lovers, with whom you found pleasure, those you loved as well as those you hated. I will gather them against you from all around and will strip you in front of them, and they will see all your nakedness.* **I will sentence you to the punishment of women who commit adultery and who shed blood; I will bring upon you the blood vengeance of my wrath and jealous anger.**

The murder of innocent children seems particularly heinous and brings the most serious Biblical punishments. Blood vengeance also must await America not only for murdering the pre-born, but also for protecting those who commit the killing.

> **Ezekiel 22:3-4, 6-9** *And say: "This is what the Sovereign LORD says:* **O city that brings on herself doom by shedding blood** *in her midst and defiles herself by making idols,* **you have become guilty because of the blood you have shed** *and have become defiled by the idols you have made. You have brought your days to a close, and the end of your years has come.* **Therefore I will make you an object of scorn to the nations and a laughingstock to all the countries...** *See how*

**each of the princes of Israel who are in you
uses his power to shed blood.** *In you they
have treated father and mother with contempt;
in you they have oppressed the alien and
mistreated the fatherless and the widow. You
have despised my holy things and desecrated
my Sabbaths.* **In you are slanderous men
bent on shedding blood;** *in you are those who
eat at the mountain shrines and commit lewd
acts."*

Ezekiel 23:37, 39 *For they have committed
adultery and* **blood is on their hands.** *They
committed adultery with their idols;* **they even
sacrificed their children, whom they bore
to me, as food for them... On the very day
they sacrificed their children to their idols,
they entered my sanctuary and desecrated
it.** *That is what they did in my house.*

Today's church has a similar problem. It is estimated
that nearly seventy percent of all women who obtain
abortions in the U.S. attend either Protestant or Catholic
churches.[7] Pro-life sidewalk counselors sadly observe car
after car adorned with Christian bumper stickers or other
symbols pulling into abortion clinic parking lots across the
country. Christians are killing their children just as the Jews
offered their precious sons and daughters to the demon idols
of the Old Testament. We have become just like our ancient
counterparts.

Isaiah 1:2-23 *Hear, O heavens! Listen, O earth!*

---

[7]An Overview of Abortion in the U.S., the Alan Guttmacher Institute,
www.agi-usa.org.

For the LORD has spoken: "I reared children and brought them up, but they have rebelled against me. The ox knows his master, the donkey his owner's manger, but Israel does not know, my people do not understand."

Ah, sinful nation, a people loaded with guilt, a brood of evildoers, children given to corruption! They have forsaken the LORD; they have spurned the Holy One of Israel and turned their backs on him. Why should you be beaten anymore? Why do you persist in rebellion? Your whole head is injured, your whole heart afflicted. From the sole of your foot to the top of your head there is no soundness – only wounds and welts and open sores, not cleansed or bandaged or soothed with oil.

Your country is desolate, your cities burned with fire; your fields are being stripped by foreigners right before you, laid waste as when overthrown by strangers. The Daughter of Zion is left like a shelter in a vineyard, like a hut in a field of melons, like a city under siege. Unless the LORD Almighty had left us some survivors, we would have become like Sodom, we would have been like Gomorrah.

Hear the word of the LORD, you rulers of Sodom; listen to the law of our God, you people of Gomorrah! "The multitude of your sacrifices – what are they to me?" says the LORD. "I have more than enough of burnt offerings, of rams and the fat of fattened animals; I have no pleasure in the blood of bulls and lambs and goats. When you come to appear before me, who has asked this of you, *this trampling of my courts? Stop bringing meaningless offerings! Your incense is detestable to me. New Moons, Sabbaths and convocations—* **I cannot bear your evil assemblies. Your New Moon festivals and your appointed feasts my soul hates. They have become a burden to me; I am weary of bearing them. When you spread out your hands in prayer, I will hide my eyes from you; even if you offer many prayers, I will not listen. Your hands are full of blood;** *wash and make yourselves clean. Take your evil deeds out of my sight! Stop doing wrong, learn to do right!* **Seek justice, encourage the oppressed. Defend the cause of the fatherless, plead the case of the widow.**

"Come now, let us reason together," says the LORD. *"Though your sins are like scarlet, they shall be as white as snow; though they are red as crimson, they shall be like wool. If you are willing and obedient, you will eat the best from the land;* **but if you resist and rebel, you will be devoured by the sword."** *For the mouth of the LORD has spoken.*

See how the faithful city has become a harlot! **She once was full of justice; righteousness used to dwell in her— but now murderers!** *Your silver has become dross, your choice wine is diluted with water. Your rulers are rebels, companions of thieves; they all love bribes and chase after gifts.* **They do not defend the cause of the fatherless;** *the widow's case does not come before them.*

This passage in Isaiah could have been written for us

today instead of to a stiff-necked people who lived 4,000 years ago. Our hands are full of the blood of millions of children and it is doubtful that God has turned His ear to hear the corporate prayers of our nation. Isaiah urges repentance to his wayward countrymen and it is still the recommended course of action for our people today. But national repentance will not come as long as God's people tolerate and, in many cases, patronize America's version of the Baal groves and World War II death camps. National repentance must begin with the individual.

However, we as individuals are prone to follow the examples set by our churches, communities, and our nation. These institutions, and most of the individuals who comprise their ranks, are in denial concerning the bloodguilt that pollutes our nation and have thus far failed to acknowledge their culpability for it. We will see, in the following chapters, how bloodguilt affects us at every level with inescapable consequences, regardless of our willingness to admit it.

This baby was aborted in the seventh month of pregnancy at George Tiller's abortion mill in Wichita, Kansas. The "partial-birth abortion" method was used.

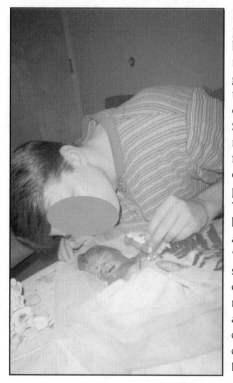

Here, the baby's father places a minature teddy bear in the hands of his murdered daughter during a greiving service provided by the abortion clinic. Seen clearly are the picture of the Sacred Heart of Jesus, representing the Catholic faith of the mother and the cross representing the protestant faith of the father. Tiller himself baptized the baby. The religious images are meant to bring "comfort" to those who shed the blood of their own children. This family later regretted their decision to abort their tiny, helpless daughter, who had been diagnosed with Cystic Fibrosis.

Part Two

The Inescapability
of
Bloodguilt

Surely for your lifeblood I will demand a reckoning; from the hand of every beast I will require it, and from the hand of man.

Whoever sheds man's blood, by man his blood shall be shed; for in the image of God He made man.

Genesis 9: 5-6

Chapter 7

*If a man strikes someone with an iron object so that he
dies, he is a murderer; the murderer shall be put to death.
Or if anyone has a stone in his hand that could kill,
and he strikes someone so that he dies, he is a murderer;
the murderer shall be put to death. Or if anyone has a
wooden object in his hand that could kill, and he hits
someone so that he dies, he is a murderer;
the murderer shall be put to death.*
Numbers 35:16-18

Personal Bloodguilt

The angry mob moved closer to the hillside where
Jesus stood praying with his disciples. Moments earlier,
Gethsemane had been the site of intense prayer between
Son and Father, but now the scene was more reminiscent of
a southern lynching. The crowd drew near to its intended
victim. Swords and clubs were at the ready while blazing
torches lit up the night sky. Jesus knew His hour had come
(Matthew 26:46).

The betrayer led the multitude to Christ and greeted
Jesus with a kiss. "Greetings, Rabbi!" he said. To this Jesus
simply replied, "Friend, why have you come?"

But before Judas could answer the loaded question,
Jesus was violently seized by the crowd and bound. Legions
of angels could have swooped down from heaven to provide
a rescue for Jesus (Matthew 26:53). Instead, Jesus allowed

this unjust treatment in order for the Scriptures to be fulfilled.

Jesus turned to give His last sermon to the multitude. "Have you come out, as against a robber, with swords and clubs to take Me? I sat daily with you, teaching in the temple, and you did not seize me." Jesus declared His innocence and their guilt.

Jesus indicted the entire crowd and implicated them in the unlawful seizure of an innocent man, yet one of the onlookers was more culpable than the rest. Judas had betrayed his Master. Judas had traveled with the disciples for years witnessing the miracles of Christ. Judas knew Jesus as well as any human could know Him. He had walked with, eaten with, and conversed with the Christ for years. Judas knew that Jesus had committed no crime, neither was any sin found in Him (Matthew 27:4).

Jesus was judicially and spiritually innocent, the perfect Passover lamb, whom Judas betrayed for thirty pieces of silver. But soon after Christ's arrest, Judas seemed to have a change of heart. The Bible recounts, *"When Judas, who had betrayed him, saw that Jesus was condemned, he was seized with remorse"* (Matthew 27:3). Judas knew the Scriptures; after all, he was one of the twelve and had even cast out demons in Jesus' name. He certainly was aware of the terrible fate of Cain, the first murderer found in the Bible. Cain's punishment was a curse and condemnation (Genesis 4:11-14). Judas must have realized his own curse was much the same as Cain's when he said, *"I have sinned by betraying innocent blood"* (Matthew 27:4).

Although Judas did not pick up a weapon and strike Jesus to kill Him, Judas was guilty of His murder. The guilt of bloodshed was applied to Judas for he was an accomplice to the murder of an innocent man. Even though Judas understood his fate, he still failed to acknowledge Christ. Unlike Peter's genuine repentance after his betrayal of Jesus (Matthew 26:75), Judas' regret was based solely on the sudden realization of the bitter consequences he must now suffer for the act of betraying innocent blood. Judas knew that Jesus was an innocent man, but failed to recognize him as the saving Lord.

The hypocritical church leaders of that day were unwilling to absolve Judas of his crime even though it was they who paid the price of blood. "What is it to us?" the chief priests asked Judas, "You see to it!" (Matthew 27:4).

Frustrated at the lack of compassion and understanding from the priests and realizing that God would still condemn him for his misdeed, Judas hurled the silver back at them. It seemed that he could not get rid of the bloodstained silver fast enough. Judas was a man so fraught with bloodguilt that Jesus aptly spoke of him when He said; *"It would be better for him if he had not been born"* (Mark 14:21).

Judas followed the advice of the priests and decided to "see to it." Burdened with bloodguilt for having betrayed Jesus to His murderers, Judas went out from the temple and hanged himself. Judas needed only to repent and he could have found the same comfort in forgiveness as Peter. Instead, he pursued death, the only solace he could find in his anguish apart from Christ. How great the sin when one must retreat into death in order to find relief!

The full hypocrisy of the chief priests is revealed in the following verses:

The chief priests picked up the coins and said,

> *"It is against the law to put this into the treasury, since it is blood money." So they decided to use the money to buy the potter's field as a burial place for foreigners. That is why it has been called the Field of Blood to this day* (Matthew 27:6-8).

The very coins that the chief priests had removed from the treasury and used to purchase the life of the Son of God were now considered unfit for the treasury. The innocent blood of Jesus had tainted them. This reveals that, not only did the chief priests understand that the death of Jesus was a murder, but that the Law of God would bring a curse on them for their participation in that murder. In a futile attempt to get rid of the evidence of their complicity and to absolve themselves of this guilt, they used the blood money for a charitable purpose, to purchase a burial field for foreigners, as if their act of generosity could possibly make up for their involvement in murder.

In the same way that the chief priests looked to deny responsibility for their participation in murder, those involved in abortion try to deny that they have any culpability in the murder of the pre-born. They even go so far as to seek to justify their wicked actions, and our culture is willing to oblige. However, the Bible says,

> *"A man burdened with bloodshed will flee into a pit; Let no one help him"* (Proverbs 28:17, NKJV).

Those responsible for innocent bloodshed should not be excused or comforted in their sin, yet, as a society, women who have abortions are treated as victims and those who support them in the decision to kill are considered heroes who were willing to stand by their friends or family member during a time of crisis. In reality, the woman is the same as a contract killer, hiring out the murder of her defenseless child, and the supporter is a co-conspirator, aiding and abetting the crime. They believe that their charitable act of lending support will some how make up for their participation in the murder. Until they can both face the fact that they bear responsibility for the murder of an innocent child and own up to it, there should be no comfort for them.

This personal dimension of bloodguilt and its effect should not take us by surprise. The Bible is full of stories that relate to this aspect of guilt. The following accounts illustrate the responsibility of the individual before God and man for the shedding of innocent blood.

◆ ◆ ◆

As Jonah's ship was being tossed to and fro by the mighty tempest, the crew considered who was to blame. When the lot fell on Jonah, he told the men that the only way to calm the sea was to throw him overboard (Jonah 1:12). Instead, the shipmates rowed even harder toward land. They did not want to have Jonah's blood on their hands and make their situation worse. They had to be sure that throwing him overboard would resolve the corporate guilt they all had for harboring a fugitive from God.

Jonah was convinced that, since he was to blame for the storm, the only way the ship would be saved would be for him to be tossed into the sea, but he was too cowardly to take the literal leap himself. The ship's crew finally realized that the only way to save the vessel was to follow the advice of Jonah. However, before they threw him overboard, they pled with God not to hold his blood accountable to them.

"We pray, O Lord, please do not let us perish for this man's life, and do not charge us with innocent blood" (Jonah 1:14 NKJV). These men knew of bloodguilt and they wanted no part in it. They completed their request for acquittal by offering sacrifices and taking vows before the Lord (Jonah 1:16). They feared the Lord, and rightfully so. Innocent blood demands a high price and these men knew the cost would be their own lives in exchange for Jonah's. Thankfully, Jonah did not die, but instead endured a life-altering humbling from the hand of God. It was only then that he was in a frame of mind that allowed him to fulfill God's will by completing the task assigned to him.

◆◆◆

David was a man who well understood blood guiltiness. Early in David's adult life, he was spared from shedding innocent blood when Nabal's wife, Abigail, came to David bearing gifts (I Samuel 25:32-33). By his own admission, Abigail saved him from the bloodguilt of avenging himself on the wicked Nabal.

◆◆◆

In order to be absolved of personal liability for accidental bloodshed, God instructs homeowners to build a wall around the perimeter of their rooftops to prevent anyone from being killed in an accidental fall. Deuteronomy 22:8 states, *"When you build a new house, then you shall make a parapet for your roof, that you may not bring guilt of bloodshed on your household if anyone falls from it."*

Ahab and his wife Jezebel conspired to murder their

neighbor Naboth. Ahab wanted Naboth's home and field for a vegetable garden. Ahab had offered a fair price or to exchange the property for a better parcel of land. But Naboth, wanting to honor God's law against selling off the family estate, refused to bargain. In order to appease her pouting husband, Jezebel hired a couple of scoundrels to report a lie about Naboth. Not only was Naboth unjustly convicted and stoned, but the rest of his family was also murdered in order to prevent any of them from inheriting the land coveted by Ahab. The full weight of guilt for the shedding of innocent blood was upon the house of Ahab.

Elijah was told to pronounce judgment upon Ahab and Jezebel, *"In the place where dogs licked up Naboth's blood, dogs will lick up your blood – yes, yours!"* (1 Kings 21:19). The stain of blood-guiltiness had invaded Ahab's home and soon he lay dead of wounds received in battle while his blood was lapped from his chariot by dogs (1 Kings 22:38). The mastermind in the murder of Naboth received her unavoidable fate soon after. Jezebel was thrown from a tower, eaten by dogs, and her body scattered in their dung across the field (2 Kings 9:36-37).

◆◆◆

The references above illustrate personal bloodguilt. How do we be relieved of it? Again in light of Scripture, it is completely reasonable to say that today bloodguilt stains the hands of all who participate in a murder, even the murder of the tiniest human baby. Bloodguilt flows from the abortionist and his staff to the mom seeking to snuff out the life of her child, as well as the friend or family member who drives her to the murder mill. The blood is red and the guilt is black as coal.

The injustice is extreme. But where is the raw outrage at this injustice? Where are the pulpits that thunder with the cry of bloodguilt, calling on their members to embark on campaigns for the God-ordained brand of justice that would cleanse our land of it? And why should the pastor speak up? He knows that those who have been affected by the shedding of innocent blood will do exactly what every other unrepentant person does whose guilt is brought to light by Scripture. They will bolt for cover to avoid the light that gives them no relief from conviction by transferring their membership to a nice church that keeps silent in the face of murder, where they can enjoy some form of unearned peace.

Where is the outrage? It is suppressed by all of us who are principals, accomplices, or complicit bystanders in this matter. The outrage is directed against those who dare to speak the truth, but does not turn inward in honest examination of conscience as a precursor to repentance.

It is no mystery that the killing fields continue to run red with innocent blood. The disgrace of bloodguilt does not stop at the murderer or the assassin, but invades our own living rooms and churches. And we play our own part to silence those who might speak up. It is personal, it is individual.

But the problem of bloodguilt goes beyond the culpability of individuals. It reaches out and encompasses the community. Like the invading storm clouds that sweep unabated across the plains, bloodguilt has swept over our land. The wind is in our face, and soon the storm's fury will be upon us. There is no way to escape the tempest and no way to outrun the rain.

However, the blood of Jesus cries out of better things

than the cries for vengeance from the innocent blood that soaks our American soil. The question is, will we, as individuals and as communities, flee to Christ for repentance and cleansing, or will we brave the billows of the storm of judgment with feigned invulnerability?

But the problem of bloodguilt goes beyond the culpability of individuals. It reaches out and encompasses the community. It is important to see God's viewpoint in the spreading of blood pollution and guilt.

Chapter 8

*See, the LORD is coming out of his dwelling to punish
the people of the earth for their sins.
The earth will disclose the blood shed upon her;
she will conceal her slain no longer.*
Isaiah 26:21

Community Bloodguilt

a group of young boys were riding their bikes
in a vacant field in Chino Hills. The dirt lot was soon to
become part of a new Southern California freeway, but today
it was a playground. The boys raced their bikes over dirt
hills and through the mud. Their boyhood curiosity led them
to explore a pile of five cardboard boxes haphazardly thrown
to the side of the newly emerging freeway construction. Like
any inquisitive boys searching for treasure, they dove into
the boxes to seek their fortune.

Peering into the cartons, their hopes of finding riches
were lost. Instead they uncovered the bloodied remains of
fifty-four pre-born children. The boys scurried home in tears,
horrified at the grisly discovery.

The police found out many months later that Albert R.
Brown, a Los Angeles abortionist, paid a driver to get rid of
the bodies instead of contracting with a nearby company for
their incineration as required by California law. The
incinerator service was expensive, cutting into his daily

profits, so Brown opted for a cheaper way of getting rid of the bodies that were stacking up in his office. The delivery driver accepted a trivial sum of money, drove two hours out of town, and cast the cadaver-filled boxes down a dirt hillside.

One week after the discovery, hundreds of people gathered at the dirt lot for a memorial service. Flowers, balloons, and cards marked the exact location of the find.

The community of Chino Hills was in emotional turmoil. How could this happen? What could be done? Who was to blame? Everyone knew abortion was a fact of life but somehow the community felt a sense of responsibility. Calls of concern flooded the local churches, but few people seemed to have the answer.

The gut feeling of responsibility shared by the community of Chino Hills, California, was an accurate one. God says that shedding innocent blood defiles the land. They were experiencing that defilement in part.

> *Do not pollute the land where you are. Bloodshed pollutes the land, and atonement cannot be made for the land on which blood has been shed, except by the blood of the one who shed it* (Numbers 35:33).

This pollution requires atonement. This is only accomplished when the murderer is brought to justice. Although Albert R. Brown later committed suicide, bloodguilt is still an issue for those who participated with him in the murders and for those that knew the murders would take place but failed to act to protect the innocent victims. This includes the State of California, which has failed to enact or enforce laws protecting the pre-born.

This is a crucial point because some people confuse a mere balancing of the external scales, (i.e., "eye for an eye"), with the justice required in Scripture to cleanse the land. The four different forms of government that God has established each have certain responsibilities and limitations. Civil justice – that is, the justice that civil rulers are to execute in behalf of the land as a whole – is not something that an individual on his own can accomplish. Families and churches do not have the authority to execute anyone or convene courts for civil justice. It is the civil authorities as representatives of the land that are given the task of avenging capital crimes (Romans 13). If they fail, then the land – the earth, the inhabitants, and the government – are not cleansed of innocent blood. Individuals, families, or churches operating on their own cannot establish justice on behalf of the civil authorities – that is, on behalf of the land. When those other than the civil government act in a way that usurps the responsibility of civil government, it does not cleanse the innocent blood but adds to it.

In Deuteronomy, Chapter 21, God outlines the proper response for putting away the guilt associated with innocent blood and defines how the civil leaders must act to purify the community. There is no individual action that will resolve the tragedy, for an innocent man is dead. But there is action that can resolve the consequences.

> *If a man is found slain, lying in a field in the land the LORD your God is giving you to possess, and it is not known who killed him, your elders and judges shall go out and measure the distance from the body to the neighboring towns (Deuteronomy 21:1-2).*

The presupposition of this passage is that if the people knew who did it, they would have turned him in. If the civil authorities knew who did it, they would have put him on trial and, upon conviction, punished him by means of execution. There would be no need for the ritual of expiation.

However, sometimes the murderer was unknown and there was no witness to the crime. In those cases, the first action after the discovery of a corpse was to determine jurisdiction. A measurement was taken from the body to determine the closest city because it was the inhabitants of that city who would be responsible for finding the murderer, putting him on trial, and exacting the required punishment.

Then the elders of the town nearest the body shall take a heifer that has never been worked and has never worn a yoke and lead her down to a valley that has not been plowed or planted and where there is a flowing stream. There in the valley they are to break the heifer's neck (Deuteronomy 21:3-4).

There is a cost to atonement. The heifer is a desirable animal for she can reproduce. A quality heifer will produce a dozen or more head of cattle in her lifetime, contributing significantly to her owner's wealth. Ranchers keep their finest cows for as long as they can to ensure a healthy herd. A young heifer nearing breeding age will bring a considerable price at any market, even today. The men bringing the animal to the valley were not responsible for the crime of murder, yet they were required to pay for it and to beg God for atonement.

Furthermore, to signify the defiling of the land, the heifer was brought into a virgin valley and slaughtered. The perfect valley was defiled, its virginity thrown away. This ritual symbolically illustrated the defilement of the crime and the appeasement of the Justice of God through the shedding of blood. This substitutionary atonement foreshadowed the work of Christ at Calvary. The ritual also included an oath to God, the community, the family, and even to the murderer that what happened to the heifer would also happen to the murderer when he was apprehended.

> *The priests, the sons of Levi, shall step forward,*
> *for the LORD your God has chosen them to*
> *minister and to pronounce blessings in the*
> *name of the LORD and to decide all cases of*
> *dispute and assault* (Deuteronomy 21:5).

The spiritual and civil leaders were called out to act in all solemnity. This was not a time for lighthearted jest. It was necessary that the ceremony prescribed by God be followed precisely and all onlookers were to observe the ritual with care. This great ordeal was to cleanse the land of the bloodguilt. All who observed this ceremony were obliged to look upon it with terror; "for the blood cries out to the magistrate for justice on the criminal, and, if that cry is not heard then it cries to heaven for judgment on the land," (Matthew Henry's commentary on Deuteronomy 21). Everyone's well-being was at stake. God's permission for them to dwell in the land was in the balance.

> *Then all the elders of the town nearest the body*
> *shall wash their hands over the heifer whose*
> *neck was broken in the valley, and they shall*
> *declare: "Our hands did not shed this blood,*
> *nor did our eyes see it done. Accept this*
> *atonement for your people Israel, whom you*
> *have redeemed, O LORD, and do not hold your*

people guilty of the blood" (Deuteronomy 21:6-8).

The leaders washed their hands over the slaughtered animal to cleanse themselves of the crime. In the same way, Pilate attempted to wash away the bloodguilt of Christ's murder when he dipped his hands in water and falsely declared that he was not responsible for Christ's death (Matthew 27:24).

As they rinsed their hands they made a very important declaration. The elders said, in essence, "We didn't do it neither did we see it! See, our hands are clean!" (Contrast this with Isaiah 1:15.) These men were making a solemn vow before God and before men that they knew nothing of the crime. They then pled with the Lord to accept the death of the heifer and their sober oath as full payment for the bloodshed. The heifer and an oath were offered in lieu of the murderer's blood with a prayer for God to expunge the bloodguilt from their heads.

> *So you will purge from yourselves the guilt of shedding innocent blood, since you have done what is right in the sight of the Lord* (Deuteronomy 21:9).

If God's redemptive plan is followed perfectly, then the bloodguilt will be removed from the land. Forgiveness will be given and the land will be purged of the pollution of innocent blood.

For example, Mrs. Ben Shalom is going about her business raising Mr. Ben Shalom's three sons and two daughters. She knows nothing about this murder, but her hands are covered with innocent blood, as are the hands of

her children and husband. Why? Because the **land** is
polluted. When the priests and Levites stand and utter the
oath that they knew nothing of it, break the heifer's neck,
and cry out to God to remove the guilt, they stand
representing her, as well as themselves. They are asking God
to cleanse her hands and the hands of her children along
with their own hands.

Today, practically speaking, we cannot break the neck
of a heifer. But our community authorities can take their
God-given responsibility to protect their citizens by diligently
conducting investigations, arresting those suspected of
murder, then executing justice through the courts. Our
religious leaders bear a Biblical responsibility to see to it that
the civil authorities act rightly. Unfortunately, our authorities
and courts have served instead to promote injustice where
the pre-born are concerned by decriminalizing abortion,
while pastors continue to conduct their affairs as if mass
murder is not occurring in their churches and communities.

Bloodguilt has an ever-expanding territory. In the
center of the circle of guilt is the person who sheds the
innocent blood. Outside that circle are his accomplices in
the murder, followed by those who may have known of it
but stood idly by and allowed the crime to happen, or did
not turn him in or rebuke him. Then come the surrounding
cities that are responsible to prosecute, but fail to, and finally
the nation, which is made up of cities whose sewers run with
innocent blood. This bloodguilt requires a reckoning with
the Lord. The transgression is between the guilty and the Creator,
but the verses of Deuteronomy 21 implicate the entire nation.

The concept of national accountability is clearly found
in Scripture. For example, when the people of Jeremiah's day
loathed his prophecy and sought to kill him, Jeremiah

responded to them by saying, *"But know for certain that if you put me to death, you will surely bring innocent blood on* **yourselves***, on* **this city***, and on* **its inhabitants***; for truly the Lord has sent me to you to speak all these words in your hearing"* (Jeremiah 26:15).

Notice the progression of culpability in this verse:

1. **Yourselves:** These were the people who would actually do the killing.

2. **The city:** Although the city is an inanimate object, like the land, it still suffers the consequences of bloodguilt. The land is defiled with the bloodshed of the innocent and cannot prosper as it should (Numbers 35:33).

3. **The inhabitants**: The citizens of the city where innocent blood is shed will be held accountable for the crime of murder whether they actually participated in the crime or not.

As the circle of liability expands, so does the responsibility for action. Ephesians 5:11 says, *"Have nothing to do with the unfruitful deeds of darkness, but rather expose them."* The converse is also true. We have fellowship with darkness if we do not oppose it. Put simply, silence is consent. Silence to Paul is refusing to expose the deeds of darkness.

Leviticus 19:17 further elaborates upon our responsibility to act: *"Do not hate your brother in your heart. Rebuke your neighbor frankly so you will not share in his guilt."* Silence in the face of sin is an expression of hatred for our neighbor. Not only that, but also this verse imputes a portion of the wrongdoer's guilt to the one who does not love enough to correct.

Community bloodguilt means that the inhabitants of a civil jurisdiction where innocent blood has been shed shoulder the responsibility for the murder until the slayer is located and properly dealt with in conformance to God's law. God holds every city throughout the world responsible each time innocent blood is shed on the land within its jurisdiction where justice has not been done by the civil representatives of that city. If the community refuses to bear that responsibility, they will bear the murder's punishment.

After Cain killed Abel and was banished by God from the land, he was afraid that someone might kill him *(Genesis 4:14).* Cain understood the proper judgment required by God for the atonement of innocent blood; *"if a man sheds blood, by man shall his blood be shed."* The rest of Genesis 4 through 9 is a commentary on what happens to society in the absence of the God-given authority to execute murderers. Genesis 6:11 introduces the flood narrative with a statement of society's failure to deal with blood-guiltiness: *"The earth also was corrupt before God, and the earth was filled with violence."* Genesis 9:6 conveys this authority to execute murderers after the flood, and is followed by a fuller statement in the Mosaic Law where the application of the Sixth Commandment is frequently expounded upon. But those first few chapters of Genesis still stand as a warning to the society that refuses to implement God's present mandate for justice in regard to innocent blood.

Two other points are noteworthy here. First, apart from God's mandate, killing in personal revenge does not answer the need for justice and cannot cleanse the land. This kind of killing only adds to the bloodguilt and the impending judgment that must come.

Secondly, bloodguilt is cumulative and cross-generational. As mentioned, the bloodguilt spreads far and wide and is not limited only to the active perpetrators of the crime. Jesus said to the Jews in Matthew 23:31-32, *"Therefore you are witnesses against yourselves that you are sons of those who murdered the prophets. Fill up, then, the measure of your fathers guilt."* The bloodguilt of every innocent murder victim from Abel to Zechariah crossed generational lines and brought judgment upon Jerusalem forty years after Jesus' proclamation of Matthew 23, and thousands of years after the original murder of Abel.

Return with us to Chino Hills to see how bloodguilt works.

Many of the women in the crowd who gathered at Chino Hills to mourn and protest the discovered bodies of the aborted children declared that one of the babies could have been her own. How sad. Somehow an antiseptic procedure in a doctor's office is acceptable, but when the baby's body is discovered lying in a field, he or she is someone to mourn. The hands of each mother and father were stained with blood. **This is personal bloodguilt.**

Every day we drive past the killing places. We carefully avert our eyes and thoughts from the gruesome reminders found in every Yellow Pages directory. If the babies' bodies do not appear in local vacant fields, then they are stacked high in bloody buckets at the local pathology labs and incinerators.[1] We steer clear of all conversation about

---

[1] George Tiller operates an industrial incinerator at the Women's Health Care Services in Wichita, Kansas. The ash of aborted baby bodies has been observed by the authors emanating from the smokestack.

abortion. We shun the opportunities to give needed advice to friends contemplating abortion. We refuse to enter into dialogue with fellow employees about child-killing. We approve with our votes politicians who support the death penalty for unwanted children while we disapprove of the death penalty for baby-killers. We criticize our pastors when they raise this issue with us. **This also is personal bloodguilt.**

Besides implicating itself in the murder, the community faced a greater problem. The citizens of Chino Hills could not follow the pattern prayer uttered by the elders over the broken heifer, if that were required today.

"Our hands did not shed this blood, nor did our eyes see it done" (Deuteronomy 21:7). Although many attending the service may have been personally responsible for slaying innocent babies, many more bore guilt in another way. They knew it was being done but they had said nothing. **This is community bloodguilt.**

Our lawmakers and judges continue to proclaim by law the right of mothers to choose to kill their children before birth. The executive office of our government, the President, the Department of Justice and all the various police forces at every level continue to defend these laws and protect the abortionists in the very act of their killing. Our pastors refuse to criticize child-killers but instead are quick to run down the sign-wielding pro-lifers who force them to look and deny what they see. **This is corporate bloodguilt.**

Both our eyes and the eyes of the families at Chino Hills see the shedding of innocent blood every day. We know where the children are dying. We know who is committing the murder. We know what day to make an appointment and what time to show up.

No longer is death meted out in the "back-alley" among the winos, drug dealers, and women of the night. Today children are murdered in fashionable locations on downtown Main Streets. The perpetrators of murder are not cowering in their sins like Cain and Judas. Instead, they flourish in our social clubs, city halls, judges' chambers, and in the halls of Congress. Some even sit as elders in our churches.[2]

Instead of handing the perpetrators over to the civil authority and demanding that justice be served, most of us are covering their sins and hiding their crimes. Our own judges and elders are not qualified to go to the virgin field to plead their innocence for they are accessories after the fact. Since we are aiding and abetting within the walls of our churches and the boundaries of our cities those who shed innocent blood, we too are guilty.

There is no need to take a measurement to the closest city for every metropolis in America is defiled by blood and no atonement has been made for over 41,600,000 dead children whose blood cries out to God for vengeance and judgment. Our hands have shed it. Our eyes have seen it. We are not innocent. Bloodguilt has polluted our land.

Yet when a pastor, like the pastors in Chino Hills, is

---

[2]Westminster Presbyterian Church of Lincoln, Nebraska, promoted abortionist Winston Crabb from deacon to elder, sparking protests from pro-life groups such as Rescue the Heartland beginning in 1997. Crabb stepped down after serving his two-year term. An article about the protests can be read on the Missionaries to the Unborn web site:
http://www.mttu.com/Articles/
Cop%20Protest%20at%20Church%20Harboring%20Abortionist.htm.

brave enough to actually pray about abortion, you will often hear him utter something very much like those words from Deuteronomy 21, vainly hoping for expiation. In response, he can only expect to hear the echo of Jesus' words of judgment 2000 years ago to a religious establishment not unlike ours: *"Therefore you are witnesses against yourselves that you are sons of those who murdered the prophets. Fill up, then, the measure of your fathers' guilt"* (Matthew 23:31-32). How do His words testify against him today? He has seen, and he knows who is committing the murders and where and when they take place. Yet he wants to pray the prayer of a righteous elder who has done all he can to stop it, when in fact he has not.

In Chino Hills, California, the community acted rightly yet missed the point. They gathered at the scene of the crime to mourn for the fifty-four babies ripped from their mothers' wombs. Instinctively, the community knew the city had been polluted by innocent blood. But in their attempt to assuage the guilt, they implicated the nation. Rather than becoming a city of refuge for the pre-born, after a few days of mourning, they continued to be a city of refuge for the abortionists. They still continue today to allow their women to go downtown to have their babies killed.

Chino Hills is just a representative community in America. What happened there is, in effect, happening all over the nation. Because of this, innocent blood continues to pollute the land. If we refuse to do right by this injustice, we leave it to God to bring His justice. Along with punishing the murderer, God will bring on all the inhabitants of the land the punishment reserved for the murderer. This is how seriously God takes this issue.

The bad news here is obvious. The forgiveness and

restoration that we desire for our cities and ourselves escapes us because we have not faced our sin and guilt in anything more than a cursory manner. To understand the community bloodguilt problem more completely, it will be instructive to look further into the principle of cities of refuge, to see what implications it has for our modern society.

CIRCLE OF CULPABILITY FOR COMMUNITY BLOODGUILT

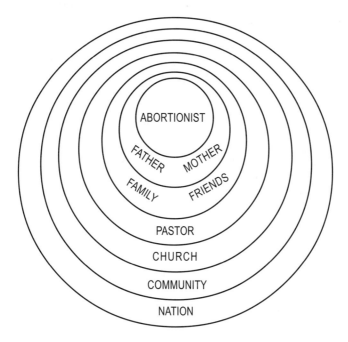

Chapter 9

Hear the word of the LORD, you Israelites, because the LORD has a charge to bring against you who live in the land: "There is no faithfulness, no love, no acknowledgment of God in the land. There is only cursing, lying and murder, stealing and adultery; they break all bounds, and bloodshed follows bloodshed. Because of this the land mourns, and all who live in it waste away; the beasts of the field and the birds of the air and the fish of the sea are dying. "But let no man bring a charge, let no man accuse another, for your people are like those who bring charges against a priest. You stumble day and night, and the prophets stumble with you. So I will destroy your mother – my people are destroyed from lack of knowledge. Because you have rejected knowledge, I also reject you as my priests; because you have ignored the law of your God, I also will ignore your children..."They will eat but not have enough; they will engage in prostitution but not increase, because they have deserted the LORD to give themselves to prostitution, to old wine and new, which take away the understanding of my people. They consult a wooden idol and are answered by a stick of wood.
A spirit of prostitution leads them astray; they are unfaithful to their God.
Hosea 4:1-12

Cities of Refuge

God's law sets up procedures for establishing justice – courts and proper authorities – so that objective justice may be established. God's heart in the matter of justice is expressed in Proverbs 17:15: *"Acquitting the guilty and condemning the innocent – the LORD detests them both."*

To protect the people from the serious consequences of injustice, God commissioned six cities of refuge to be perpetual cities of justice. The cities of refuge were originally six cities given to the Levites as their inheritance in the place of an equal share of the Promised Land. These Levites and Priests were the spiritual leaders in Israel and were also the primary dispensers of judgment. The cities were set up as a beacon of judicial equality whose purpose was twofold: they were to be sanctuaries of protection for the innocent and bastions of judgment for the guilty.

A city of refuge was a place in which a manslayer, someone that accidentally killed a man, could run to and secure his safety until such time as a full trial and investigation could be completed. A manslayer was not considered a murderer and his life was not necessarily required in judgment for the accidental death of another. Justice – not merely the death of another, even the killer himself – had to be established to cleanse the land and balance the scales. This could be accomplished only by following due process. Death for death was not sufficient to establish justice.

Deuteronomy 19:4-6 gives a hypothetical scenario for the use of the Cities of Refuge.

> *For instance, a man may go into the forest with his neighbor to cut wood, and as he swings his ax to fell a tree, the head may fly off and hit his neighbor and kill him. That man may flee to one of these cities and save his life* (Deuteronomy 19:5).

This was to prevent his unnecessary death at the hands of the "avenger of blood," the next of kin to the deceased who was charged with seeking retribution on behalf of his dead family member. Although the avenger of blood had every right to kill the manslayer outside the sanctuary of the cities of refuge, once inside, the killer's life could not be legally taken without an investigation and hearing. This was to prevent the needless shedding of blood by the angry and grieving family of the dead victim whose emotional state may not allow for them to consider the extenuating circumstances of their loved one's death. The cities of refuge prevented unnecessary bloodshed and helped to curb the blood feuds between families that often arose from accidental deaths, thus protecting the land from the shedding of innocent blood.

Even in the matter of the "avenger of blood" there was due process. The avenger could not be just anyone. It was a requirement that the avenger be the next of kin to the slain victim. Anyone else who took matters into his own hands and killed the manslayer would become guilty of murder, even if the manslayer otherwise legally deserved to die.

In today's economy, there is no longer a place for the avenger of blood because, throughout America, the laws insure protection to the accused. "Innocent until proven guilty" is a Biblically-based principle of law that, from a practical standpoint, makes every American city and town a city of refuge. Under the Old Testament economy, the avenger of blood would bring bloodguilt upon himself if he slew a man who had fled to a city of refuge. In the same way, an individual, regardless of any kinship claims, would today be legally responsible for taking a life in retribution in the United States.

The cities of refuge were safe havens for the innocent.

However, if a man intentionally murdered another, the cities of refuge, (and the horns of the altar in Jerusalem, a similar refuge mentioned in I Kings 1:50), were no safe haven for him, but were a place of judgment and death.

> *But if a man hates his neighbor and lies in wait for him, assaults and kills him, and then flees to one of these cities, the elders of his town shall send for him, bring him back from the city, and hand him over to the avenger of blood to die. Show him no pity. You must purge from Israel the guilt of shedding innocent blood, so that it may go well with you* (Deuteronomy 19: 11-13).

The cities of refuge were fortresses of righteousness and justice, keeping the people undefiled from the guilt and judgment of innocent blood. Joab found this out when Solomon had him dragged from the altar and executed for his murders (1 Kings 2).

The most important application of the city of refuge principle is Deuteronomy 19: 7-10.

> *This is why I command you to set aside for yourselves three cities. If the LORD your God enlarges your territory, as he promised on oath to your forefathers, and gives you the whole land he promised them, because you carefully follow all these laws I command you today – to love the LORD your God and to walk always in his ways – then you are to set aside three more cities.* **Do this so that innocent blood will not be shed in your land,** *which the LORD your God is giving you as your inheritance, and* **so that you will not be guilty of bloodshed.**

Although our government structure is significantly different from Israel's theocracy, the spiritual leaders of our nation bear a Biblical responsibility to stand as a beacon of light and protection, instructing the nation concerning God's standards of right and wrong, and providing a safe haven of refuge for the innocent. At the same time, it is the responsibility of our civil leaders to protect the innocent from injustice by executing justice upon the guilty and carrying out righteous judgment.

Our civil and religious authorities today would profit from a serious study of the Biblical principles of bloodguilt and the cities of refuge as they offer important insight into the nature of justice. Until protections for the lives of the pre-born are insured, God will continue to detest the nation that acquits the guilty and condemns the innocent. But let us go on now in the study of bloodguilt, to examine how this principle applied in New Testament times.

Chapter 10

For he who avenges blood remembers; he does not ignore the cry of the afflicted.
Psalm 9:12

Bloodguilt in the New Testament

The doctrines of innocent blood and bloodguilt are woven like scarlet ribbons throughout the pages of Scripture from Genesis to Revelation. Although people in ancient days only had access to bits and pieces of God's mighty Word, they still exhibited a firm grasp on the doctrine of innocent blood. Since today's Christians have the entire canon at their disposal, there is no reason for ignorance of these important Biblical concepts.

There is ample scriptural evidence that the people in Jesus' day had a working comprehension of bloodguilt. Even Pontius Pilate, a Roman, understood this concept and attempted to avoid it as he washed his hands in a futile attempt to rid himself of that guilt as he turned Jesus over to the will of the murderous mob.

The religious leaders, also, not only understood bloodguilt but also chose to warp the doctrine to suit their inclinations. They were unwilling to accept a refund of Judas' coins, contaminated with the betrayal of Christ's blood, or put them back into the treasury because they understood that the coins had officially become blood money. Though this scruple is ironic in the extreme, (in line with their false understanding of oaths, Matthew 23:16-22), it nonetheless demonstrates a keen, if self-indicting, understanding of innocent blood.

The bloodguilt Israel incurred by executing first the prophets, then Jesus Christ, and later the Apostles and other believers, resulted in a disaster for the nation of Israel in 70 AD. Jesus prophesied this disaster in Matthew 23 and 24 when He pronounced the seven "woes" upon the nation of the Jews. They refused to admit their need for atonement by something more effective than bulls, goats and lambs (Hebrews 10:4). In their refusal, they chose bloodguilt for themselves.

As in the days of Gideon, Elijah, and Ezekiel, the Jews of Jesus' time made idolatry the order of the day. The Jewish religion had perverted itself to the extent that they missed the very point of the law, which God had revealed to them. Jesus had strong words for the bloodguilty hypocrites of his day.

> *"Woe to you, teachers of the law and Pharisees, you hypocrites! You give a tenth of your spices – mint, dill and cumin. But you have neglected the more important matters of the law – justice, mercy and faithfulness. You should have practiced the latter, without neglecting the former"* (Matthew 23:23).

After a lifetime of reading Moses, as well as three years of watching Jesus, listening to His preaching, and observing His miracles, the Jews should have known better than to reject Jesus. If the scribes and Pharisees had any tenderness in their hearts toward God, they would even have been able to foretell the very day of Christ's visitation from the Scriptures they pretended to hold so dear. But alas! Instead of embracing them, Jesus cast curses upon the phony religious leaders who should have realized that this was the hour of their redemption.

His indictment against Israel turned on the issue of bloodguilt:

> *Woe to you, teachers of the law and Pharisees, you hypocrites! You build tombs for the prophets and decorate the graves of the righteous. And you say, "If we had lived in the days of our forefathers, we would not have taken part with them in shedding the blood of the prophets." So you testify against yourselves that you are the descendants of those who murdered the prophets. Fill up, then, the measure of the sin of your forefathers! You snakes! You brood of vipers! How will you escape being condemned to hell? Therefore I am sending you prophets and wise men and teachers. Some of them you will kill and crucify; others you will flog in your synagogues and pursue from town to town. And so **upon you will come all the righteous blood that has been shed on earth, from the blood of righteous Abel to the blood of Zechariah son of Berekiah**, whom you murdered between the temple and the altar. I tell you the truth, all this will come upon this generation* (Matthew 23:29-36).

This was the last and final "woe" of the seven "woes" pronounced upon the unrepentant nation. In two more verses Jesus said to them, "*Look, your house is left to you desolate.*" It was a fatal matter for Israel to reject the truth and turn aside from their God. Their rejection continued the pattern of spilling innocent blood, because when they killed Christ but refused to admit their guilt, they rejected the innocent blood of a better covenant: "*by so much more Jesus has become a surety of a better covenant*" (Hebrews 7:22).

Hebrews 8:6-7 builds on this idea: "*But now He has obtained a more excellent ministry, inasmuch as He is also Mediator of a better covenant, which was established on better promises. For if that first covenant had been faultless, then no place would have been sought for a second.*"

Then in the last verse of Hebrews 8, the author restates the superiority of the New Covenant in Christ: "*In that He says, 'A new covenant,' He has made the first obsolete. Now what is becoming obsolete and growing old is ready to vanish away.*"

There is still a desperate need for someone to pay the bloodguilt of God's people (Matthew 23), since Biblical justice demands it. The writer of Hebrews drives this point home when he says in 12:18-25 that in the church we do not come to the *pattern* of things revealed on the mountain – blood, thunder, and fire which can only condemn us, not save us – but rather, we come to the *reality* to which that pattern pointed. We come "*to Jesus the mediator of a new covenant, and to the sprinkled blood that speaks a better word than the blood of Abel. See to it that you do not refuse Him who speaks. If they did not escape when they refused Him who warned them on earth, how much less will we, if we turn away from Him who warns us from heaven?*" (Hebrews 12:24-25).

The innocent blood of the New Covenant in Christ has the power to atone for all the innocent bloodshed from the beginning of time to the end, and to purify the whole earth – the land. Rejecting that innocent blood is to reject the only standard that is effective against innocent bloodshed, excluding the lawful execution of the murderers, which is commanded by God in Scripture.

Israel made a practice of murdering the prophets sent by God to warn her of sin and idolatry. Jesus pointed this out to the teachers and pastors of the day. In Matthew 23, He then predicted the coming martyrdom of the future saints as well as His own death on a cross, due to happen in just a few days (Matthew 23:29-36).

At the end of Matthew 23, Jesus announced that the time for mercy was over. The innocent blood from the first murder victim, Abel, until the prophet Zechariah, was crying out to God continually from the days of their untimely deaths. Now there would be a reckoning. It was time to settle the scores. There would be hell to pay one way or another! Either Christ's blood would satisfy justice in their place, or they would pay the penalty for innocent blood themselves.

Many of the saints of God, of both the Old and New Covenant, are under *"the altar who had been slain because of the word of God and the testimony they had maintained"* (Revelation 6:9). It is their innocent blood howling for vengeance, crying to God, *"How long, Sovereign Lord, holy and true, until you judge the inhabitants of the earth and avenge our blood?"* (Revelation 6:10).

We piously recall the saintly last words of Stephen in Acts, *"Lord, do not hold this sin against them"* (Acts 7:60). We forget that in the Revelation of Jesus Christ to John, we see Stephen praying one more time under the altar, *"How long . . . until you . . . avenge our blood?"*

Jesus was telling the teachers and priests that He had heard the cry of innocent blood and soon it would be the time for vengeance. *"It is mine to avenge; I will repay. In due time their foot will slip; their day of disaster is near and their doom rushes upon them"* (Deuteronomy 32:35).

"I tell you the truth, all this will come upon this generation" (Matthew 23:36). In 70 AD, Jerusalem was completely annihilated, bringing that generation to a close, even as Jesus promised. Not a stone of the temple was left on top of another (Matthew 24:2). The sacking of the Holy City was complete – a physical reality correlating with the spiritual reality taught by the book of Hebrews: no Temple, no altar, no sacrifice, no ashes of purification, no priesthood. Not even today, two thousand years later, have the Jews been able to reestablish Mosaic worship. The brutal destruction of Jerusalem and dispersal of the Jews was, according to Jesus, God's judgment for the shedding of innocent blood!

Having heard of Jesus' pronouncement against them, the Jews desired to have Him quickly killed. After His arrest, Pontius Pilate attempted to have Jesus released because innocent blood was a concern to him, but the priests and elders had incited the Jewish crowd to demand that Barabbas be freed and Christ crucified.

> *"Why? What crime has he committed?" asked Pilate. But they shouted all the louder, "Crucify him!" When Pilate saw that he was getting nowhere, but that instead an uproar was starting, he took water and washed his hands in front of the crowd. "I am innocent of this*

> man's blood," he said. "It is your
> responsibility!" All the people answered, "Let
> his blood be on us and on our children!"
> (Matthew 27:23-25).

The people had cursed themselves. They knew innocent blood was going to be shed; they had demanded it. Furthermore, they testified against themselves, even insisting that the pure blood of Jesus Christ be accounted to them and their children in a way that would guarantee judgment on themselves and their progeny.

Before the final retribution would befall Jerusalem for centuries of accumulated bloodguilt, the acts of the apostles, especially Peter, illustrate further how bloodguilt affected the Jews and their ability to receive the gospel.

The Apostles, after Christ's death and resurrection, preached the Good News to all who would hear, but many did not want to listen. The day of Pentecost had come. God's people had been filled with the Holy Spirit. From that time on, the Apostles no longer hid in a room but zealously took the message of life directly to the people in the city and countryside.

Soon jealousy arose in the sect of the Jews called the Sadducees. The Sadducees arrested the Apostles and threw them in jail as recorded in Acts 5. This did not slow the disciples from preaching their controversial message. The Angel of the Lord delivered the Apostles from jail and gave them specific orders, saying, "Go, stand in the temple courts and tell the people the full message of this new life." The miraculous jailbreak infuriated the Jewish leaders so the officers were called to once again gather the men and bring them before the Sanhedrin council.

*Having brought the Apostles, they made them appear before the Sanhedrin to be questioned by the high priest. "We gave you strict orders not to teach in this name," he said. "Yet you have filled Jerusalem with your teaching and are **determined to make us guilty of this man's blood**." Peter and the other Apostles replied: "We must obey God rather than men! The God of our fathers raised Jesus from the dead – whom you killed by hanging Him on a tree"* (Acts 5:27-30).

The priests and elders were troubled about the innocent blood of Jesus Christ. They had hoped that once Jesus was dead and buried everyone would forget about their crime of murder. On the contrary, Christianity was spreading like wildfire and the major doctrine of the new faith was Jesus' innocent blood, which alone had power to atone for the sins of the world. Their fears had borne fruit, and their sin had been exposed. The orders given to the Apostles were clear enough: stop preaching Christ crucified. Stop implicating the priests and elders in the crime of murder.

Peter's answer to the Jewish leaders is the same one many Christians give today when told to stop preaching the Gospel. *"We must obey God rather than man."* The Gospel often brings a conviction leading to repentance and a new life. Sometimes it brings conviction leading to the hardening of the sinner's heart and his striking back at the preacher. The certainty of jail time and death did little to deter the Apostles as they boldly preached the Gospel message and reprimanded the Jewish leaders for their misdeeds.

Religious leaders have changed little over the past

2,000 years. Today, they are among the most offended when the simple truth of abortion is depicted and people are urged to flee to Jesus Christ for healing and atonement. Where our sin, even the sin of bloodguilt, is proclaimed, the innocent blood of Christ, our only hope, is also declared. This is, after all, the true Gospel.

Anyone who opposes this message would seem to stand in a long and dishonorable tradition. Yet church leaders today are in the forefront of pleading with Christians to stop showing pictures of aborted babies because they might offend someone and give their churches a bad name. In 1991, the well-known Pastor Charles Stanley, of the 10,000-member First Baptist Church of Atlanta, expressed with disgust his feelings about active pro-life work to Rev. Joseph Foreman, one of the founding leaders of Operation Rescue. "The problem with y'all is that they tar all of us with the same brush with which they tar you!" he said. And Stanley is not alone. The majority of religious leaders seem quite unconcerned for the children being murdered each day as a result of pastoral apathy.

These church leaders want Christians to stop implying that the Church has any responsibility for abortion, because, in the leaders' view, teaching against abortion is too political, and the implication of human sacrifice is not theologically apt. Like the religious leaders of Jesus' day, they tell us, you "are *determined to make us guilty of this man's [the babies'] blood.*" With this argument against showing the blood of the children and the setting forth of Scripture's case for the bloodguilt of the Church, they hit a biblical stumbling block: *"I tell you the truth, whatever you did for one of the least of these brothers of mine, you did for me"* (Matthew 25:40). The basis of the declaration of guilt against the Church lies in its inability to see the face of Christ in the face of those who are murdered. They cannot see their way through to deal practically with abortion as the murder of innocent children created in God's image. This same blindness to Christ brought His final judgment against the leaders of Jerusalem: *"You snakes! You brood of vipers! How will you escape being condemned to hell?... And so upon you will come all the righteous blood that has been shed on earth... I tell you the truth, all this will come upon this generation"* (Matthew 23:33-36).

The real problem with exposing child-killing and bloodguilt in the world is that it is the Church that opposes and obstructs the teaching – sometimes viciously. The pastors and church leaders sense their own guilt and the extent to which tearing down the altars of Baal begins in the sanctuary of the Lord (1 Peter 4:17). That is evident in the lip-service many pro-lifers have received when discussing abortion with their pastors. Most church leaders steadfastly refuse to accept the responsibility they know they must accept, choosing instead to disallow obedience while pretending to be without spot. When those few Christians do stand to hold the church accountable, the pastors make every attempt to dismiss them as fools or "whackos." Thank God for those who say with sincere humility, *"We must obey God rather than man."*

In all, the doctrine of innocent blood was clearly understood by the people of the New Testament. But now, in America, we have the bloodshed of over 41,600,000 children crying out to the Lord continually for vengeance. Will its ferocity match the judgment poured out upon Israel in 70 AD? If the 41,600,000 children murdered in the U.S. by abortion since 1973 have anything to say about it, the answer is certainly, "Yes!"

The innocent blood of these children cries out in the same way that the martyrs under God's throne plead continually for justice: *"How long, Sovereign Lord, holy and true, until you judge the inhabitants of the earth and avenge our blood?"* (Revelation 6:10).

Those who say in spirit and in truth, "Blessed is He who comes in the name of the Lord," will ask for the perfect and innocent blood of Christ not only to atone for them, but also to transform them into people who do their part in His name to bring an end to the shedding of innocent blood. Those who emulate the Pharisees and reject the teaching of Christ in their hearts, in spite of what they outwardly say or do, can only cling to the false hope that perhaps God will not notice the blood that stains their hands.

As we will show, the guilt of murder lies not just upon the hand of the killer, but on the hands of all who are involved when murder has been committed.

Troy Newman kneels in prayer as he preaches a message of repentance outside a "pro-abortion" church service held during the 2000 Democratic National Convention in Los Angeles, California.

Newman leads Christians in an imprecatory prayer for repentance and justice outside Reformation Lutheran Church in Wichita, Kansas. Late-term abortionist George Tiller is a member there.

Part Three

Whose Responsibility
Is It, Anyway?

Thus says the Lord: "Execute judgment and righteousness, and deliver the plundered out of the hand of the oppressor. Do no wrong and do no violence to the stranger, the fatherless, or the widow, nor shed innocent blood in this place."
Jeremiah 22:3

You shall not murder.
Exodus 20:13

Chapter 11

*But righteous men will sentence them to the
punishment of women who commit adultery and shed
blood, because they are adulterous
and blood is on their hands.*
Ezekiel 23:45

The Murderers Among Us

In the mid-1990's, a murder plot was revealed in
the military town of Oceanside, California. Camp Pendleton,
a military instillation located on the northwest border of San
Diego County, is nestled next to the city of Oceanside, a
community bordered by the beautiful Pacific Ocean. It is a
city tailor-made for Marines who are off duty.

The inviting commercial district and beach party
ambience entices military personnel to come spend their
weekends and paychecks in this sunny seaside village. On
Friday nights, Oceanside is awash in a sea of buzz haircuts.
Young men in the prime of their military conditioning cruise
the streets searching for a thrill even greater than firing fully
automatic machine guns and driving tanks in the Southern
California desert. These men know how to live life on the edge.

Downtown Oceanside is a short two blocks from the
beach and consists of bars, strip clubs, and tattoo parlors; it
is a cornucopia of worldly recreation. For a young man from
a small Midwest town, the beach combing, bar-hopping, and

loose women are an irresistible combination. The sounds of music and laughter fill the summer night air and the drinking and carousing in the surreal semitropical atmosphere can sweep away all sense of restraint like the evening tide washes away footprints in the sand.

The sordid love triangle played itself out on the beach of Southern California and the Camp Pendleton Marine base. A young Marine and his bride, a fun-loving girl from back home, had come to the seaside station, but for different reasons. He had come to serve his country; and she had married a soldier hoping for travel and escape from the boring small town life.

All too soon, her new life with her husband was becoming more and more dull. He did not want to stay up all night drinking and dancing. There was school, studies, and duty to which he must diligently attend. His plans for the future did not revolve around a bottle of tequila and a sunset; so, for reasons still not completely understood, she sought to have him murdered.

She did not need to look far to find willing accomplices in her murder-for-hire scheme. Two of her husband's best friends had noticed his all-too-obvious dedication to duty and honor, to the neglect of his family. While he spent more and more time attending to his career, perhaps as an escape from an unhappy home life, his companions began to spend more time entertaining his bored wife. She pilfered the thousand dollars they had been saving toward a down payment on a house and approached the buddies to strike a deal. The men hesitated at first but soon found themselves discussing with interest the details of the prearranged assassination. Finally, the men agreed to kill the husband for a mere thousand dollars. At the last minute, she threw in a few sexual favors just to sweeten the deal and assure their participation.

Thankfully, "Operation Seek and Destroy," as they called it, was never executed. A plot as sinister as this was hard to conceal and the MP's broke up the conspiracy before it could be brought to fruition. At the ensuing trial, finger-pointing was the order of the day. She blamed the men involved while they blamed her and each other. In the end, all three were found equally guilty and sentenced to equal jail terms.

If anyone found it odd that the woman who merely hired the assassins was treated with the same culpability as the men willing to lie in wait to murder a friend, no one rose to voice an objection. The general consensus was that this was a righteous decree by the civil magistrate.

There was no outpouring of public concern from the community declaring her a victim of society. There were no help centers set up to give aid to all the future contract killers so that they might find alternatives to murdering their husbands. The churches did not welcome her on the condition that neither of the parties would discuss the crime. There was no legislation brought forward by the National Organization for Women to pardon her and all future murderesses. There was no sympathy publicly expressed for her – only the satisfaction that comes from witnessing justice.

Why, then, do we consider any differently the women who seek to hire killers to murder their pre-born children? Why the hesitancy to say that not only the mothers, but also the fathers who willfully abort their babies, are guilty of murder? Why is there such outrage expressed at the notion that those who know of the crime but do not intervene, like most of the churches in America, share a portion of the guilt?

Who holds the fathers, the mothers, the neighbors, the pastors, and the bystanders guilty? Who would dare?

God can! God does!

God not only holds them accountable, He expects a just society to implement laws to hold them accountable also:

> *For he [the government] is God's servant to*
> *do you good. But if you do wrong, be afraid,*
> *for he does not bear the sword for nothing. He*
> *is God's servant, an agent of wrath to bring*
> *punishment on the wrongdoer* (Romans 13:4).

By comparing abortion directly to any other act of premeditated contract killing, it is easy to see that there is no difference in principle. However, in our society, a mother of an aborted baby is considered untouchable where as any other mother, killing any other family member, would be called what she is: a murderer.

If abortion is murder, should we not act like it?

We cannot claim to be obedient Christians while willfully ignoring the innocent blood that is shed in our communities by those who live next door or sit next to us at church each Sunday. We become guilty of the shedding of innocent blood when we excuse it by refusing to call it what it is.

Chapter 12

*ou, therefore, have no excuse, you who pass judgment
on someone else, for at whatever point you judge the
other, you are condemning yourself, because you who pass
judgment do the same things. Now we know that God's
judgment against those who do such things is based on
truth. So when you, a mere man, pass judgment on them
and yet do the same things, do you think you will escape
God's judgment? Or do you show contempt for the riches
of his kindness, tolerance and patience, not realizing that
God's kindness leads you toward repentance? But because
of your stubbornness and your unrepentant heart, you are
storing up wrath against yourself for the day of God's
wrath, when his righteous judgment will be revealed.*
Romans 2:1-5

Moms Who Murder

Often our experiences with our children teach
lessons about spiritual matters in unexpected ways. So it
was with the Rev. Joseph Foreman, who shared about an
encounter with one of his daughters to illustrate an important
spiritual truth.

> With irrefutable logic, zeal, panache,
> and vigor I closed my lecture to my wayward
> child. She was shouting and bossing around
> her little brothers, getting them to do the work
> that was rightfully hers, and she had been

warned before. This time I had been trying to concentrate, and there she was again. She was wrong, red-handed, open and shut. I caught her at it. When it was over, in tears she said to me, "But, Dad, all I did is what you did yesterday when you lost your temper at Mom and had to apologize to us."

She was right. Of course, this did not justify her actions, but she defended them nonetheless. She was simply crushed by my inconsistency. What struck me was the transgenerational consistency of the situation. She was growing up to be just like me. It is so easy to see the faults of others and miss your own. My first reaction was to regret having punished her. How could I with my own guilt?

On the other hand, my guilt did not lessen her guilt. As a parent, I realized that if she was to be helped, she still needed to see her guilt as much as I needed to see mine. So I began by confessing my sin again, and then we continued to talk about her treatment of her brothers and her responsibilities."

In the story above, Rev. Foreman indicates that his own guilt over having been a poor example to his daughter caused him to think twice about disciplining her for a fault he recognized in himself. In fact, his daughter learned the bad behavior from observing him. Fortunately, his ability to humble himself and repent for his culpability in her wrongdoing led to a productive teaching time that benefited them both.

Our churches experience a similar situation when it comes to dealing with the woman who aborts her child. We hesitate to call her a murderer when, in fact, we all share a certain culpability in the crime. However, unlike the example above, Christians have exhibited a reticence to humbly confess their sin as it relates to abortion, preventing correction, and ultimately healing, from coming to the woman who has aborted.

In our current social climate, it is acceptable to lay blame for abortion at the feet of the abortionists, the social liberals who encourage the abortions, and the law-makers who allow and even pay for them. But the mother is the one person we are not allowed to call guilty. Ironically, she is the one who needs most to see what she has done.

Even in the pro-life movement, rescuers, those who take direct action to save a life, want to call abortion murder, but they are hesitant to call the mother a murderer to her face for fear of offending her and the "politically-correct" crowd. By confronting the woman with her sin, our objective is to get her to see the evil that has resulted from her actions. By withholding truthful confrontation from her, we prevent her from being brought to repentance and ultimate restoration.

It is worth listening again to what God says:

A man tormented by the guilt of murder will be a fugitive till death; let no one support him (Proverbs 28:17).

I will sentence you to the punishment of women who commit adultery and who shed blood; I will bring upon you the blood vengeance of my wrath and jealous anger (Ezekiel 16:38).

Church elders, pastors, and evangelists are refusing to give godly counsel to women who have murdered their babies, and much less to the fathers. These "fugitives" fill our pews every Sunday and are given aid and comfort instead of a call to repentance. In actual fact, they are being encouraged by the church to avoid repentance because the congregation refuses to call sin a sin. Thus, the matter is swept under the rug, leaving the spiritual wounds of abortion to fester. These guilty men and women involved in abortion are running from their sin, literally for their very lives, and the help they have supposedly found in our churches is, in truth, a contravention of God's order.

It is time to focus on the enormity of the sin of abortion and what God says about the matter. Forgiveness can be found, but only after true repentance! Paul said that God's law was a schoolmaster that leads a sinner to Christ. We must use the law as expressed in the Sixth Commandment, *"You shall not murder" Exodus 20:13*, to bring the knowledge of sin (Romans 7:7), and heighten conviction to bring those stained with the guilt of abortion to the cross of Christ.

Yes, we must confess our guilt as a society, as churches, as families, and individuals, but finally Mom and Dad involved in an abortion must be willing to say, "I am responsible for the murder of my own child. I have sinned against God and beg forgiveness through Christ's blood." Only then can Christ's saving blood begin to atone for the child-murder committed by our sisters and brothers in Christ. Likewise, only when our church leaders confess with a repentant heart their responsibility for abortion, due to their lack of leadership and teaching, can our churches be purged of their bloodguilt in the matter of abortion.

Instead of crocodile tears, we need true repentance

and that requires a change of mind about the sin of abortion and our apathy toward it. Church leaders and congregations cannot say they are sorry only to return to "business as usual" as far as abortion is concerned. They must not only forsake their sin but must also begin to walk in Biblical obedience and start speaking for those who cannot speak for themselves and rescuing those being taken away to death.

We must stop helping the fugitive find peace with her choice to murder her baby. Instead, we must direct her to seek atonement for the sin of shedding innocent blood in humble repentance through the blood that speaks a better word than that of Abel's. The price of genuine peace is owning up to the guilt and coming clean.

But there is another portentous aspect to the sin of abortion that just the obvious violation of the Sixth Commandment, which has been discussed thus far. In addition to murder, abortion is also a form of idolatry and is a transgression of the First Commandment that was imparted by God to Moses.

Chapter 13

*They sacrificed their sons and their daughters to demons. **They shed innocent blood, the blood of their sons and daughters**, whom they sacrificed to the idols of Canaan, and the land was desecrated by their blood.*
Psalm 106:37-38

Baal is Alive and Well on Planet Earth

Most Christians remember Gideon as the great judge of Israel who, against impossible odds, defeated the mighty Midianite army with a band of three hundred men. Few think of Gideon in the days before God called him to lead his people to freedom from oppression, when he threshed wheat in a winepress, a frustratingly futile task since the wind cannot freely blow away the chaff. Gideon fearfully engaged in this labor-intensive activity so the Midianites would not discover him and steal his family's meager supply of food.

In those days the Lord had given Israel over to their wicked enemies, the Midianites, the Amalekites, and other people of the East. These antagonists ravaged the countryside, destroying every living thing in their path including crops, livestock, and people. Every time the subjugated Israelites planted a crop, the Midianites would come to raze the produce before it could yield fruit. God's people lived in caves and the clefts of rocks to hide themselves from the troublesome Midianites. But their tremendous suffering at the hands of Israel's evil oppressors was truly the mighty hand of God's judgment brought upon His people because of their sin and rebellion (Judges 6:10). Revelation 6:15-16 relates a similar moment in history.

> *Then the Kings of the earth, the princes, the generals, the rich, the mighty, and every slave and free man hid in caves and among the rocks of the mountains. They called to the mountains and the rocks, "Fall on us and hide us from the face of Him who sits on the throne and from the wrath of the Lamb."*

The wrath of God was unleashed upon the nations in Revelation because of the souls crying under the altar of God for vengeance. *"How long Sovereign Lord, holy and true, until you judge the inhabitants of the earth and avenge our blood?"* (Revelation 6:10). These saints under the altar of God were crying out for the wrath of the Lamb to be poured out upon their slayers. Their blood, like the blood of Abel, is ever before the throne of God, begging the Lord for vengeance from the grave, just as Abel's blood cried out from the ground.

In Gideon's day, God was using the Midianites as a tool of destruction in His hand to bring a rebellious nation back into conformity to His divine purpose. God explains why the calamity had come upon the land of Israel in Judges 6:1: *"Again the Israelites did evil in the eyes of the Lord . . ."*

To find the source of this terrible evil we need not look any farther than the house of Gideon. Gideon was born for such a time although even he was not completely convinced of it. As Gideon threshed his wheat God told him, *"The Lord is with you, mighty warrior."* Gideon, who cowered in the winepress only long enough to get a small ration of food that was to be squirreled away from the sight of the enemy, might have thought God was talking to someone else.

Instead Gideon complained, *"If the Lord is with us then why has all this happened to us?"* Gideon knew perfectly well why God had broken them with a rod of iron. He lived his life surrounded by the idol gods and the worship abominations that went along with them. He must also have understood that God chastens the ones He loves as a father disciplines his children. God loved Israel enough to issue correction to a people straying far from His precepts. The Lord had brought the Midianites in to chasten His people until they cried to Him for deliverance. Unlike the people of the earth in Revelation, the Israelites of Gideon's day had learned from the hand of discipline. In their repentance, some were praying to the Lord for redemption (Judges 6:6).

Hence, Gideon was chosen by God to be the general in charge of rescuing the nation of God. However, before Gideon could draw his sword, before his small but mighty army could defeat the Midianite oppressors, before he could rescue God's chosen people, and before it was possible for him to be seated as Judge over Israel, God wanted him to settle matters in his own house. It was a rescue operation that had to start at home.

The justification for the Lord's chastisement of Israel was the national commission of an unspeakable evil. Israel, in Gideon's day, was chasing after the heathen idols of Baal and Ashtoreth, false gods whose worship rituals required the innocent bloodshed of human child sacrifice. These were false fertility gods of sex and immorality.

The people of God should have known better. They had been given the Law of Moses that not only forbids idolatry and murder, but defines the covenant relationship of marriage as well as the penalties for indulging in sexual trysts outside the context of God's mandates. Deuteronomy 7:12-13 promised that God would provide the blessings of fertility both in agriculture and in the family to those who walked in obedience to Him. The Israelites were well aware that no human sacrifice was permitted. But instead of honoring the sacrificial system ordained by God that would foreshadow Christ, the perfect and final sacrifice, the children of God were now shedding the blood of their own babies in an insane effort to pacify Baal, a demon idol sculpted with their own hands.

The very concept of child sacrifice is a counterfeit from the pit of hell. It is a cruel and evil mockery of the atoning work of the Son of God. Satan, who has been a liar and murderer from the beginning (John 8:44), takes pleasure in the murder of the innocent as a sacrifice that has no power to redeem but can only corrupt, bringing down the wrath of God upon those who would be deceived thereby. His counterfeit worship found a stronghold in Israel, which readily embraced his enticing forgery in the place of God's redemptive plan.

Furthermore, the Israelites knew that any form of human sacrifice was an abomination to the Lord God as evidenced in the following words spoken to Moses by God:

You shall have no other gods before me. You shall not make for yourself an idol in the form of anything in heaven above or on the earth

*beneath or in the waters below. You shall not
bow down to them or worship them; for I, the
LORD your God, am a jealous God, punishing
the children for the sin of the fathers to the
third and fourth generation of those who hate
me, but showing love to a thousand
generations of those who love me and keep
my commandments...You shall not murder*
(Exodus 20: 3-6, 13).

*Say to the Israelites: "Any Israelite or any alien
living in Israel who gives any of his children to
Molech must be put to death. The people of
the community are to stone him. I will set my
face against that man and I will cut him off from
his people; for by giving his children to Molech,
he has defiled my sanctuary and profaned my
holy name"* (Leviticus 20:1-3).

Molech was yet another in a string of false deities
requiring the blood of children to appease Satan's appetite
for innocent blood. It seems Satan has always wanted the
blood of children. The Enemy tried to kill Moses before he
was born, requiring that all the Jews to murder their own
male children by throwing them into the Nile. The Enemy
also tried to kill Jesus by moving Herod to murder all the
male children under three years old. Throughout history the
Enemy has been known to take the innocent blood of every
boy or girl he can get, whether it is through Baal worship or
abortion.

Within the property lines of Gideon's own home was
an altar to Baal, a half man, half bull king god of the ancient
Phoenicians. Next to it was a wooden Ashtoreth pole, a phallic
symbol bespeaking their profligate sexuality. These obscene

idols became as revolting to Gideon as they are to those today whose minds have been cleansed by the only true and redemptive blood sacrifice. The Lord ordered Gideon to dispose of the sin in his own house before he could deliver the people out of bondage. Gideon was required to cleanse his own hands before he could be allowed to lead the Israelites into battle to dispense God's righteous judgment upon the wicked oppressors. Only then would he be qualified to chastise Midian and liberate his people.

The demands of the Lord upon Gideon were unalterable. His obedience had to be swift, for the duty of warfare would soon follow. Gideon was to take his father's second bull and sacrifice it to the Lord. But the command was even more rigorous. Gideon must tear down Baal's altar and use the wooden Ashtoreth pole as firewood to burn that bull upon the very place where children had been slaughtered. The symbolism was clear: there was only one God, and He would not tolerate impostors. In an act of poetic justice, God instructed Gideon to destroy the demon idols in the same way that children had been sacrificed in fiery flames to Baal and his female consort, Ashtoreth.

In spite of a face-to-face conversation with the Angel of the Lord, Gideon remained fearful. He gathered ten servants and secretly crept up to the high place in the dead of the night. He destroyed the altar of Baal and rebuilt a proper altar to the Lord using the Ashtoreth pole as kindling wood, and sacrificed the bullock to the Lord.

Unfortunately, the townspeople and his own family wanted Gideon's head. The men of the city demanded that Gideon be killed for desecrating the very location where they murdered their sons and daughters. How dare a young upstart like Gideon interfere with their god of ritualistic sex and child sacrifice! The crowd grew hostile and shouted all the more for the blood of Gideon: "He must die!"

One must wonder why God would want to deliver such a corrupt band as the Israelites from the invading horde of Midianites. A father's love for his children prevailed for Israel and also in the case of Gideon. Gideon's father, Joash, made supplication for his son's life.

Joash pleaded with the vicious crowd that demanded his son's demise, *"Are you going to plead Baal's cause? Are you trying to save him. . ? If Baal really is a god he can defend himself when someone breaks down his altar"* (Judges 6:31). Joash persuaded the mob not to kill his son, and in turn the throng of idol worshipers renamed Gideon lest anyone forget what atrocities he committed. They named him Jerub-Baal, which means literally, "Let Baal Contend With Him."

Gideon went on to be a man of valor. With God's help, he defeated the horde of Midianites and drove them from the land. He restored proper worship to the Lord and sat on the Judge's seat all the days of his life. These deeds of Gideon are often recalled. They are taught to schoolchildren. They are the subjects of sermons. However, rarely are the first exploits of the mighty warrior Gideon mentioned when Jerub-Baal opposed the culture built upon illicit sex and did away with child sacrifice in the land, thus completing and illustrating God's redemptive plan for the whole earth.

The correspondence to today's society is striking. Our American culture figuratively worships at the altar of Baal and Ashtoreth. It rabidly promotes and defends with religious fervor a corrupt lifestyle of illicit sex, then aborts the offspring that results, sacrificing them, as it were, upon the altar of "convenience" as the sacrament of "Choice."

The argument can be logically made that abortion is a sacrifice to demons. The evil spirits to which children were sacrificed in the Baal groves are probably the same ones hanging out down at the Planned Parenthood offices! *"No, but the sacrifices of pagans are offered to demons, not to God, and I do not want you to be participants with demon"* (1 Corinthians 10:20).

Today, those who should be engaging the culture of death are threshing wheat in a winepress. The men of God are gathering in churches and Bible study groups, too afraid to confront the Midianites who are laying siege to our countryside. The nation is being ravaged by a horde of thieves and murderers. Our government school system has been invaded by Midianites who are razing our crops before the children have a chance to bear fruit. The Midianites are encamping all around us, desecrating our land with drugs, homosexuality, pornography, lewdness, foul language, anti-God legislation, prostitution, idolatry, and divorce. They are killing off and stealing every good thing. The enemies of the Lord encircle our churches while we are huddled inside, fearful to step out and drive the wickedness from our land.

The first step for Gideon in ending the invasion of Midianites was to cleanse his own house. The blood of innocent children occupies our own houses. We must tear down the altar of Baal and burn the Ashtoreth pole before we can attempt to conquer the invading armies.

The church in the twenty-first century travels by land and sea to plant missionaries. They are sent to China, Russia, South America, and Africa to convert the heathen masses, while back home the idol groves flourish. We cannot hope to win on the spiritual battlefield until we deal with the Baal worship within our own homes and in our own land.

Women, young and old, sit next to us in church every Sunday bearing the stain of innocent blood. Next Saturday, the abortion clinic will be full of girls sacrificing their babies to Baal and Molech. According to the Alan Guttmacher Institute, nearly seventy percent[1] of them will be from our churches!

Baal, Molech, and Asthoreth are a thriving part of the amoral culture of modern America. Today we call these same false gods the "sexual revolution" or "recreational sex", while we have renamed their sacrament of child sacrifice, "Choice," "Right to Decide," and "Reproductive Freedom." But the age-old lie is still the same.

Where are the Jerub-Baals willing to defeat the enemy within our own houses? Who could be named among us "Let Planned Parenthood Contend With Him?" Where are the mighty warriors called by the True God to defeat the enemies? Who is willing to first cleanse his own house? Oh, how the Lord searches the earth seeking those who will serve Him! But before we go to conquer the Enemy or before we can earn the privilege of sending out missionaries world-wide, we must contend with the blood-stained altars to the false deities that demand child-sacrifice within our own homes and churches and cities.

Yes, Baal and his acolytes are alive today and doing quite well on Planet Earth. As Baal worshipers filled Israel with sexual immorality and child sacrifice, Planned Parenthood and others of their ilk fill America with worship to the idols of the sexual revolution and abortion. In the same way that Israel was polluted with innocent blood,

---

[1] An Overview of Abortion in the U.S., the Alan Guttmacher Institute, www.agi-usa.org.

America and the Church are defiled and cursed with the innocent blood of aborted children. The people of Israel refused to rebuke those who sacrificed children to Baal. Today, the Church refuses to confront those who abort their children to the same of spirit of Baal. Christians seem shocked when they read that the apostate Israelites allowed Baal worship even in the temple of God, all the while Planned Parenthood board members are allowed sit as elders in some of our churches.[2] This is the height of hypocrisy!

Not much has changed in 3,000 years. As Solomon said in the book of Ecclesiastes, *"There is nothing new under the sun."* The name of Baal has changed to Choice but the act is the same and so are the results. Dead babies defile our land and God is furious. We must expect to suffer the same consequences as that of Old Testament Israel – complete annihilation – if we as a culture and civilization reject such commandments of our God and Creator, as *"You shall not murder."*

Our nation today needs more Gideons to lead it back to God's righteous standards. Thankfully, the Scriptures tell us of men and women of faith who stood strongly as God's prophets, bringing their nations to repentance. We can and must follow their examples.

---

[2] A cursory inspection of the Internet immediately revealed dozens of people who serve or have served as both as church elders and Planned Parenthood board members. Here are five: **D. Bruce Roberts**, Indianapolis, Indiana, ordained elder, North United Methodist Church; **Naomi Aiko Yamashiro**, Kailua, Hawaii, elder of the Kailua Seventh-day Adventist Church; **Nina Mills**, Flint, Michigan, served as a deacon, elder and trustee for her church, First Presbyterian Church; **Lerold W. Chase**, Raleigh, North Carolina, former Pastor Central Presbyterian Church, Buffalo, New York, where he also served on Planned Parenthood's Board of Directors; **Erica Lynn Horn**, Frankfort, Kentucky, sat on the board of Nathaniel United Methodist Mission while serving as board member at her local Planned Parenthood.

Chapter 14

The kings of the earth did not believe, nor did any of the world's people, that enemies and foes could enter the gates of Jerusalem. But it happened because of the sins of her prophets and the iniquities of her priests, who shed within her the blood of the righteous. Now they grope through the streets like men who are blind. They are so defiled with blood that no one dares to touch their garments.
Lamentations 4:12-14

The Prophets of Baal vs. The True Prophets of God

Queen Jezebel.

The name conjures up images of evil, wickedness, and immorality. Jezebel was the epitome of sin and vice. The daughter of the pagan king, EthBaal the Sidonian, Jezebel married King Ahab of Israel. This was an unholy alliance forbidden by the Law of Moses (Deuteronomy 7:2-3). Jezebel brought into the land a mingling of worship of the one True God and the counterfeit divinity, Baal, whose pagan ritual of child sacrifice filled the land. Her reign of terror is analogous to the fictional queen in the C. S. Lewis novel, *The Lion, the Witch and the Wardrobe*, where the White Witch turned all who opposed her into stone. Any creature that dared mention the name of the great King Aslan would instantly suffer her ire.

Queen Jezebel, along with her 450 prophets of Baal

and 400 prophets of Ashtoreth, reestablished government-sanctioned child killing in the northern nation. The true prophets of God naturally opposed such a heinous crime. Like Lewis' White Witch, Queen Jezebel murdered anyone who dared to speak the name of the Lord or prophesy God's true Word (1 Kings 18:4). Consequently, much innocent blood was shed throughout the Northern Kingdom. The land was defiled and the guilt of innocent bloodshed was upon all the inhabitants of Israel.

The prophets of God were scattered throughout the countryside. Some hid in caves while others cowered in fear for their lives in valleys and ravines. Jezebel was bent on obliterating all who opposed her religion. Since speaking out against the killing of children meant certain death for a man of God, few dared to try. Of course, those who silently conformed to the hideous practices of Jezebel's abominable demon idols were accepted as perfect subjects under the depraved King and Queen.

Thank God for the prophet Elijah. He was a man's man, clothed roughly in camel hair and willing to speak out against the sin of the nation. At the onset of Ahab and Jezebel's wicked reign, Elijah pronounced God's discipline on the apostate nation. He called upon God to smite the land with a horrible drought, so that not a drop of rain fell on Israel for three years. Even though every man, woman, and child suffered under the curse of God because of the bloodshed, the people did not depose the malevolent Ahab and Jezebel, neither did they turn back to the God of their forefathers. Instead, they continued in their worship of Baal and Ashtoreth, committing lurid sex acts then killing babies to appease their newfound gods.

In order to win the people back to the true God of

Israel, Elijah prepared a great contest between the rival gods (1 Kings 18:16-45). Huge crowds gathered to witness the spectacle, much as fans today would watch two popular prize fighters battle for the heavyweight crown. The prophets of the idol, Baal, numbered 450, while Elijah solely represented the God of Israel. Speaking through their prophets, each god insulted the other. The Baal prophets wildly chanted and danced while slashing their bodies until blood flowed profusely from their wounds. When there was no apparent response from the demon god, Elijah mocked Baal saying, "Maybe Baal is sleeping, shout louder!" The match persisted all day with the "baby-killers" clearly running out of steam (and blood) toward evening.

Elijah took the fight to the people. *"How long will you waver between two opinions?"* he asked, speaking of the age-old struggle of Baal vs. God. *"If the Lord is God, follow Him; but if Baal is god, follow him"* (1 Kings 18:21). The people stood in mute indecision. (Could they possibly have been contemplating their great sin of child-sacrifice?)

The people were being forced to make the same decision that God had put before their forefathers so many years ago at Mount Sinai.

> *This day I call heaven and earth as witnesses against you that I have set before you life and death, blessings and curses. Now choose life, so that you and your children may live and that you may love the LORD your God, listen to his voice, and hold fast to him. For the LORD is your life, and he will give you many years in the land he swore to give to your fathers, Abraham, Isaac and Jacob* (Deuteronomy 30:19-20).

At the end of the day God easily prevailed in a display of His power and authority, sending down fire from heaven, and burning Elijah's proper animal sacrifice as well as the many gallons of water with which it had been doused. God is a consuming fire[1] and His Spirit cannot be quenched! The King of Kings and Lord of Lords brought clear and utter defeat to those who promoted the shedding of innocent blood.

When the people saw God in action they fell on their faces and cried out, *"The LORD – He is God! The LORD – He is God!" (1 Kings 18:39).*

Elijah completed the victory by cutting off the heads of the 450 false prophets who had advocated child sacrifice, and bringing at least partial justice to a land that had been devoid of it for years. Furthermore, with the Lord's people once again acknowledging Him, God unleashed the rain clouds from a three-year hiatus. Justice had released the land from the blood curse, according to Genesis 9:6, *"Whoever sheds the blood of man, by man shall his blood be shed; for in the image of God has God made man."*

Although the people had repented, the infuriated Jezebel and her husband, Ahab, remained firmly entrenched in power. Jezebel was bent on recommencing her wicked religious practices throughout the land. Understanding that Jezebel would demand vengeance for the lives of her fellow false prophets, Elijah fled into the desert in despair.

While Elijah was in hiding, he called out to God, *"I have been very zealous for the Lord God Almighty. The Israelites have rejected your covenant, broken down your altars, and put your prophets to death with the sword. I am the only one left, and now they are trying to kill me"* (1 Kings 19:14).

---

[1]Hebrews 12:29

The Great and Awesome God of the Universe would have none of Elijah's whining. God told him to go back to work and anoint Jehu as a new king over Israel. Furthermore, He corrected Elijah's notion that he was alone in the world. *"Yet I reserve seven thousand in Israel – all whose knees have not bowed down to Baal and all whose mouths have not kissed him"* (1 Kings 19:18). Elijah, now confident that God would complete the good work He had started, set out once again to confront the wicked King and Queen.

Ahab was soon killed in battle and, just as Elijah prophesied, dogs licked up the King's blood from the bottom of his chariot. Jezebel's child-killing career lasted much longer. Her tenure spanned from 1 Kings 16 to 2 Kings 9. She controlled the kingdom through the short reigns of Ahaziah and several others, all the sons of Ahab. But in the end she was thrown from a high tower by two eunuchs and her body was eaten by dogs and scattered in the fields through their excrement. Only her hands, feet, and skull were left behind from the canine feast (2 Kings 9:35). It seems that even the dogs hate the hands that shed innocent blood (Proverbs 6:17), feet that run swiftly to shed innocent blood (Romans 3:15), and a mouth that speaks insolence against God (Romans 1:28-32).

The modern day application is more than apparent. Abortionists and "safe sex" proponents are as the prophets of Baal and Ashteroth. Jezebel rules in Congress, Planned Parenthood, and in many of our churches. In Revelation 2:20, Jesus rebukes the church of Thyatira for tolerating *"that woman Jezebel"* and her teaching of *"sexual immorality."* Then, as now, sexual immorality leads to child killing. The spirit of Jezebel, embodied in the widespread practices of recreational sex and abortion, is prosperous here in the United States and the Baal/Ashtoreth trade – as reflected in pornographic films, books, videos, TV, magazines, and the Internet – is big business.

◆◆◆

Christians are only too happy to look aside when it comes to child-killing, and in many ways are like the people in Israel who went along with the government-sanctioned Baal worship. We kill children from conception through birth and it is all authorized, endorsed, legitimized, paid for, and protected by Uncle Sam. When a true prophet makes a stand, he or she is promptly silenced. To that end, the federal government has made the "rescue" of children a federal crime under the Freedom of Access to Clinic Entrances Act (F.A.C.E.), punishable by jail time, huge monetary judgments, or both. Many who once came to the rescue now cower in the desert whining with Elijah, "We tried and we were broken."

Our churches are hardly different. When a Christian speaks out in a congregation against the Baal of our times, he or she is discretely invited to find the door. Pastors who should be encouraging their congregations to stand against the wickedness of child-killing are instead strangely silent, refusing to preach the whole counsel of God. They seem to prefer peaceful coexistence with the abortionists rather than to stand against them and risk unpopularity, or worse, a drop in the weekly offerings. In some ways, the church today is a kind of Thyatira; the New Testament Israel is tolerating that woman Jezebel.

We build crisis pregnancy centers next to abortion mills, then think our job is done.[2] We have built the altar of

---

[2] See Appendix D: "Why Supporting a Crisis Pregnancy Center is Not Enough."

God next to the altar of Baal. We are tolerating the intolerable, hoping God will not notice that we have failed to tear down the heathen altar and have no other Gods before Him. The church in America must be asked, *"How long will you waver between two opinions? If the Lord is God, follow Him; but if Baal is god, follow him"* (1 Kings 18:21).

Just as Elijah acted in faith against great odds to conquer the child sacrificers of his day, so, too, can today's people of God step out in faith, trusting that God will work through them to end the shedding of innocent blood. As in the past, God has and will continue to anoint His chosen people to overcome evil and stand in faith. Those who have gone before serve as our examples and our inspiration. It is time to come out of the desert as Elijah did and speak the word of the Lord in faith, recognizing that victory is inevitable.

By faith Noah was warned about an impending judgment and built an ark to save his family (Hebrews 11:7).

By faith Moses' parents defied the law of Egypt and rescued their son from death, setting him adrift in the Nile where he was discovered and adopted by a princess (Hebrews 11:23).

By faith Moses forsook the treasures of Egypt to be identified with the suffering of Christ (Hebrews 11:24-26).

By faith the Israelites escaped Egypt and walked on dry land through the Red Sea while the waters swallowed up Pharaoh and his army behind them (Hebrews 11:29).

By faith the prostitute Rahab defied the law in Jericho and rescued the spies from the law enforcement officials (Hebrews 11:31).

"And what more shall I say? I do not have time to tell about Gideon, Barak, Samson, Jephthah, David, Samuel and the prophets, who through faith conquered kingdoms, administered justice, and gained what was promised; who shut the mouths of lions, quenched the fury of the flames, and escaped the edge of the sword, whose weakness was turned into strength; and who became powerful in battle and routed foreign armies. Women received back their dead raised to life again. Others were tortured and refused to be released, so that they might gain a better resurrection. Some faced jeers and flogging, while still others were chained and put in prison. They were stoned; they were sawn in two; they were put to death by the sword...

Therefore, since we are surrounded by such a great cloud of witnesses, let us throw off everything that hinders and the sin that so easily entangles, and let us run with perseverance the race marked out for us. Let us fix our eyes on Jesus, the author and perfector of our faith..." (Hebrews 11:32-12:2 abbreviated)

Even now, God has reserved for Himself thousands who have not bowed their knee to Baal. They are fighting the battle against idolatrous child sacrifice at this very moment. Today, men and women are in the trenches of the abortion war while much of the church cannot even discern the sound of battle raging in their own neighborhoods. God has set aside His "seven thousand" and many are not hiding in caves. They are fighting, not for their own lives yet, but for the lives of the tiny babies. They are fighting in faith.

Edith, in faith, traveled three thousand miles to fast and pray for three days at the steps of the Supreme Court. By faith, this eighty-year-old woman refused to bow to tyranny and went to jail for a day when the court created a new law that day, just for her, forbidding her from holding a sign begging protection for the pre-born.

By faith, Gary stood at Planned Parenthood day after day patiently pleading for the babies even though his health had been seriously deteriorating for ten years. Even now, after a liver transplant, he continues to stand for the pre-born.

By faith, Joe spends at least three days a week parked in front of an abortion clinic praying for the needs of the children and their mothers.

By faith, Cheryl has faithfully counseled women at her local abortion clinic for over nineteen years every Saturday, rain or shine, and by faith she has spared hundreds from execution.

By faith, Jeff spent a total of one year in jail for refusing to leave the doors of abortion clinics.

By faith, Connie invested over ten years of her life standing against abortion. She now continues to help children by operating an orphanage in Tijuana.

By faith, Joseph suffered through jail, persecution from the state, and lies from the media only to be ordered by an unjust court to pay Planned Parenthood $109 million as a penalty for his impudence in standing against abortion, finally driving him to bankruptcy which even then left intact the judgment against him.

By faith, Ron, enduring angry motorists and harassment from police officers, drives his sign-laden vehicle from coast to coast, just so people will see his message and perhaps not kill their babies.

By faith, Tom refused to conform to the liberal Lutheran acceptance of abortion and lost his pastorate rather than compromise God's Word.

By faith, two small children and their mother working next to an abortion clinic in Dallas, Texas, reached out in love to Jane Roe of Roe v. Wade Norma McCorvey, and won her heart for the Lord.

By faith, Al preaches every Sunday to a small congregation filled with pregnant women from the maternity home he founded after his former congregation left when he began to preach against the sin of abortion.

By faith, Mark blocked the door of an abortion clinic in order to save a life and was given a week in jail, after which he lost his job.

By faith, Bob refused to leave the door of an abortion mill where a doctor was waiting to kill children. He was sprayed repeatedly with mace by the L.A.P.D. while handcuffed, in retaliation for his selfless act.

By faith, Ken sacrificed his wealth in order to save babies, only to be incarcerated in a mental hospital for a month by a local abortionist. He has been arrested and sued but, by faith, he represents himself in court so he may personally testify to police and judges of the Lord Jesus Christ, rather than find a lawyer, who though more versed in law, would not see this opportunity to represent Jesus Christ.

By faith, Joe has worked tirelessly for three decades to find new and creative ways to stop abortion and close abortion mills only to be sued by the National Organization for Women (NOW). By faith he refused to bow to judicial tyranny and has put up his family's home as an appeal bond, trusting that God will either give him victory over the enemy or provide for his needs in persecution. Finally, as a result of faith, he won the lawsuit before the United States Supreme Court, and secured freedoms for all pro-lifers.

By faith, thousands upon thousands laid down their lives for the precious babies at the doors of abortion clinics. By faith, they acted like abortion was murder. By faith, they endured beatings and abuse. By faith, some served short jail terms, others long months behind bars. Many, by faith, suffered the loss of friends, churches, and great sums of money. But by faith, abortion clinics were closed, families were spared the loss of their children, and abortionists were converted by the Gospel of Christ.

Through faith, by running the race Jesus has laid out for His people, Christians will win the abortion war and send the likes of Jezebel back to the pit of hell. The innocent blood demands a reckoning. The prophets of Baal will meet their fate in the hands of God but it is up to God's people to stand, like Elijah, and oppose the child killing. It is only through faithful obedience of God's people in exposing this abomination that Jezebel will be thrown from her high tower of influence and the innocent blood will stop flowing in the streets of America, averting the inevitable judgment that God will bring upon those who condone murder.

Chapter 15

*H*e answered me, "The sin of the house of Israel and
Judah is exceedingly great; **the land is full of bloodshed
and the city is full of injustice**. They say, `The LORD has
forsaken the land; the LORD does not see.' So I will not look
on them with pity or spare them, but I will bring down on
their own heads what they have done."
Ezekiel 9:9-10

The Judgment of Innocent Blood

*I*nnocent blood and judgment are inexorably linked.
When innocent blood is shed, justice in some form must
certainly follow. It is essential to the immutable order of God.
After Timothy McVeigh was found guilty of murdering one
hundred and sixty-eight people, he suffered the full
punishment for his crime when he was executed six years
after he blew up the Murrah Federal Building in Oklahoma
City. The justice of God had then been satisfied for his part
in the shedding of innocent blood. In McVeigh's case the
civil magistrate acted Biblically to cleanse the land of the
bloodguilt. God's order of law requires that the person
directly responsible for murder should pay with his life, lest
the land and its inhabitants be brought under the heavy hand
of the Lord (Deuteronomy 21).

Regrettably, there is nothing being done today to
expunge the bloodguilt for the babies being murdered in
abortion mills. Their innocent blood is ever before the throne

of God and their persistent voices plead with Him for vengeance in a manner similar to the cries of the martyrs under the altar of God: *"How long, Sovereign Lord, holy and true, until you judge the inhabitants of the earth and avenge our blood?"* (Revelation 6:10). Sooner or later, the Lord will answer their cries and take that burning coal from atop the altar of God and hurl it to earth in retribution for the innocent blood (Revelation 8:5).

This scenario has been played out over and over throughout Biblical history. The United States is guilty of innocent blood. The question is not, "Will God judge?" but rather, "When will His righteous judgment fall?" Billy Graham's wife, Ruth, once made an acute observation to the effect that if God does not judge the United States, He will have to apologize to Sodom and Gomorrah.[1] In the same way, God would also have to apologize to Israel for the righteous judgments brought upon that nation if He does not judge America for the sin of abortion. Since no such apology is likely to be forthcoming from the righteous King of the Universe, it appears that judgment for America is a foreseeable inevitability.

It is possible that America is already within the clutches of remedial judgment. One needs only to analyze the current societal dilemmas to see the hand of God moving upon our land. The historical record of the Bible shows that God chastens before He sends cataclysmic destruction.

Although the United States is not Israel, she is a nation founded upon God's Laws more than any other country since

---

[1]Although Ruth Graham originally made this observation to her husband, Billy Graham has publicly repeated it and it is often attributed to him.

Israel. America's forefathers covenanted with God for His blessings in return for their obedience. Since she has been at least partially in compliance with His will, she has benefited from the blessings of the Lord, which He has poured out upon this nation. These blessings include relative wealth, luxury, and security. In spite of this, America continues to rebel against God's laws in social matters, primarily sexual morality and abortion. Because of God's patience with the United States, she is not languishing in ruin at the bottom of the ocean today, as are the cities of Noah's era. God has displayed long-suffering and mercy, but now the Lord's hand is reaching down from heaven to touch the soil and inhabitants of America. He is warning this nation, preparing her for a day of reckoning.

The social ills of our day have not grown to plague our society overnight. The drug epidemic, once troubling only a fringe of our society, is now claiming the lives of our young and old, destroying families and taking a dramatic toll on our nation. School shootings, where children murder other school-age children, once shocked Americans, but now have become nearly commonplace and hardly worth much mention on the evening news. Unbridled pornography along with all the filthy sexual deviance associated with it has grownn from the back-alley peep shows into an industry of filth that now ranks among the top money-producing businesses in our nation.[2] It has been generally conceded that it is not the First Amendment, but pornography that has been the driving force behind keeping the Internet free of any censorship. Divorce, marital infidelity, and rebellious children were once a source of shame to American families, but are now considered the standard way of life. Terrible violence, from rape to road rage, is infecting America. Most

---

[2]Enough is Enough, Alarming Facts, http://www.enough.org/.

recently, America has been the target of unprecedented terrorist attacks on her own soil that have killed thousands and adversely affected the once strong American economy. In all of these, it may be that God is showing that His hand of protection is being withdrawn.

There is good reason to believe that the root cause of droughts, floods, and wildfires is not global warming but God's discipline on a rebellious nation stained with bloodguilt. AIDS, cancer, mutated antibiotic-resistant bacteria, and other plagues meet the criteria for being judgments from God (Deuteronomy 28:27). Since Scripture tells us that God places wicked people to rule over nations that are in rebellion to Him, wicked leaders and ungodly Congressional officials are manifestly a judgment from the Lord. God is also attempting to capture this nation's attention by affecting something American's hold dear – their pocketbooks. These warnings manifest themselves in the forms of high taxes, inflation, skyrocketing energy costs, and an unstable stock market, in order to induce our stiff-necked people to cry out to God in repentance for deliverance.

God holds the entire cosmos in His hand (Isaiah 40:12), and He directs everything (Romans 8:28). People simply cannot be allowed to dismiss as happenstance the corrective disciplines the Lord is using to bring about a wide-scale revival in this country. The truth must be told! God wants America to turn back to Him, but just like Israel, whose stubborn, sinful behavior required God to bring ruin to the nation, America may also be facing final and total destruction.

The entire Old Testament, especially the book of Judges, warns that it is God's way for nations that will not heed His warnings, to hand them over to the brutalities of the oppressors. America, so proud and secure in her military might, thumbs her nose at God. She has wrongly believed that no power could touch her shores, although the terrorism of 9-11 has taught her better.

There can be no doubt that the oppressor is being prepared by the hand of God. Will it be the Islamic jihad that hates everything about America, especially her Christian heritage? Or will it be China, whose billion-man military might, U.S.-derived nuclear technology, and ballistic missile capability are foolishly dismissed as holding any significant threat to our national security? Perhaps the oppressor will instead be a world organization such as the pro-abortion United Nations, which has worked for years, openly and behind the scenes, to erode the national sovereignty of its member nations while consolidating power and amassing an army in its own name. Maybe the oppressor will take the form of financial ruin. Whatever the case, judgment may not be far off.

When decisive retribution finally fell upon Israel through the Babylonian captivity and destruction of Jerusalem, it was, in part, for the shedding of innocent blood. Israel was utterly destroyed and the people were scattered throughout the world. Again, the second destruction of Jerusalem in 70 AD was largely due to the shedding of innocent blood, Christ's blood included (Matthew 23:37-38). If God so judged His chosen people, it is unrealistic for the Church in America to think that God will spare her, who has shed more innocent blood than Israel ever could.

America, including God's people who dwell there, is under a curse from the Lord today, but her people refuse to recognize God's hand in the matter. Watching television and making "weekend get-a-ways" in SUVs have become obsessive national pastimes by which a self-absorbed people can distract themselves from having to consider God's chastening. Like Israel prior to the Babylonian captivity, America ignores God's warnings, dismisses the prophets, persecutes those who act upon their beliefs, and denies her corrupt and dangerous state.

> *If at any time I announce that a nation or kingdom is to be uprooted, torn down and destroyed, and if that nation I warned repents of its evil, then I will relent and not inflict on it the disaster I had planned. And if at another time I announce that a nation or kingdom is to be built up and planted, and if it does evil in my sight and does not obey me, then I will reconsider the good I had intended to do for it* (Jeremiah 18:7-10).

America looks prosperous and healthy at first glance, but inwardly she is poor, wretched, blind, and naked. She has sown to the wind like a disobedient child who thinks there are no consequences for her actions, not realizing that her parent approaches with a paddle. Like the church of the Laodiceans in Revelation 3:14-22, this nation would do well to buy a salve for her eyes so that she would be able to see. *"Those whom I love I rebuke and discipline. So be earnest and repent"* (Revelation 3:19).

The question remains: what can be done to rectify the situation that looms so ominously before our nation – a desperate condition due in large part to our national implication in the murdering of innocent pre-born children? In His mercy, God does offer us a remedy that we can put into practical effect.

Chapter 16

*Therefore as surely as I live, declares the Sovereign
LORD, I will give you over to bloodshed
and it will pursue you.*
Ezekiel 35:6

The Proper Reaction to
Innocent Blood

Before God vented His wrath on His stiff-
necked and rebellious people during the first destruction of
Jerusalem, the prophet Ezekiel was given a vision foretelling
the judgment about to come upon the land. He was at home
enjoying the fellowship of his friends, a group of the elders
of Judah, when God grabbed him by the hair and lifted him
up into heaven. It was here, recorded in chapter eight of
Ezekiel's book of prophecies, that he was shown why
Jerusalem was to be destroyed.

Ezekiel was shown the sins of the people. The vision
revealed an Idol of Jealousy and the seventy elders of the
house of Israel offering incense to false gods. Women were
weeping for the Babylonian fertility god of Tammuz while
men were prostrating themselves to the sun in the East. God
rhetorically asks Ezekiel several times, *"Do you see these
things?"* God tells Ezekiel that these acts are not trivial
matters, but are detestable in His sight. Furthermore, God
rightly accused the apostate Israel because they had filled
the land with innocent blood.

It was an indictment against the people of God – the chosen ones. He had brought them up from the land of Egypt and given them the land flowing with milk and honey. God had warned them repeatedly that if they followed after false gods and shed innocent blood that the land would vomit them out as it had the former inhabitants. God made it clear that the Israelites did not inherit the land on the merits of their righteousness but rather because the Canaanites had become detestable to God. They had brazenly committed abominable acts of sin, rebellion, and murder (Leviticus 18, especially vv.20-28).

Now in Ezekiel's vision, it was clear that God had intended to make good on His promise to bring His wrath upon Jerusalem for all Judah's abhorrent sin and bloodshed. In Ezekiel 9, the vision is played out further. God calls in a loud voice for the angels of judgment to appear before Him. Six angels of vengeance were summoned, each bearing an axe ready for slaughter. Mercifully, with the angels was another type of angel, standing alone and clothed in white linen. He bore on his side a writing instrument. God instructed this angel to go down to earth before the axe-wielding angels and seek out the people that God would spare from the impending slaughter.

God instructed this angel to place a mark on the forehead of all the men, women and children who belong to the Lord. These were the citizens of Heaven, the ones who had a heart for God. Today we might call them "real Christians" or the Invisible Church.

The mark on the forehead spoken of in Ezekiel 9:4 was a life-saving brand, for God then commanded the other six angels to follow the first angel *"through the city and kill, without showing pity or compassion. Slaughter old men, young men and maidens, women and children, but do not touch anyone who has the mark. Begin at My sanctuary"* (Ezekiel 9:5).

The mark on a person's brow was akin to the blood on the door frame in Exodus 12:23: *"When the Lord goes through the land to strike down the Egyptians, he will see the blood on the top and sides of the doorframe and will pass over that doorway, and He will not permit the destroyer to enter your house and strike you down."*

In Revelation 7:3, God places a similar mark on the foreheads of His people just before He smites the land in judgment. God commands, *"Do not harm the land or the sea or the trees until we put a seal on the foreheads of the servants of our God."* This mark was to differentiate between good and the evil persons, the redeemed from the cursed. Revelation speaks also of another mark, the mark of the beast. That mark is the counterfeit of God's mark and will condemn a man to eternal death, but the mark of God upon the forehead will set people apart for eternal life. These marks suggest that the ones in covenant with and in service to God will be as obvious to the world as a visible brand on the face.

In Ezekiel's day, in order to receive the life-saving mark on the forehead from God, one had to meet His strict criteria. How would the angel know whom to mark? The angel with the ink pen was told to *"Go throughout the city of Jerusalem and put a mark on the foreheads of those who **grieve** and **lament** over all the detestable things that are done in it"* (Ezekiel 9:4).

The individuals saved from the axe-wielding angels were the persons crying and weeping over all the terrible sins of the land. These two words translated "grieve and lament" are also translated "sigh and cry." They are some of the most passionate words used in the Old Testament. Other words that might be used today are wail, howl, bemoan, weep, and mourn. These are powerful words, flowing from our innermost being, that describe a strong emotional outcry against heinous sin.

These virtuous men and women revealed their heart for God by hating the wickedness and bloodshed in the city just as much as God did. This wailing and bemoaning of the detestable acts against God's order and authority were tears leading to life. Jesus promised to those who were poor in spirit and mourned that they would be comforted by the Kingdom of Heaven, and that out of them would come springs of water welling up to eternal life (Matthew 5:3-9; John 4:13-14).

When the final Babylonian judgment came upon Jerusalem, few were spared. However, men like Daniel, Shadrach, Meshach, and Abednego were not harmed. They had sighed and cried for the sins of their people, so God saved them from the wrath that fell swiftly on those who were unconcerned for the things of God. The vision of Ezekiel, as it took place in Heaven, was played out physically in the book of Daniel, Chapter 1, and also in 2 Kings 24:1-7.

> *During Jehoiakim's reign, Nebuchadnezzar king of Babylon invaded the land, and Jehoiakim became his vassal for three years. But then he changed his mind and rebelled against Nebuchadnezzar. The LORD sent Babylonian, Aramean, Moabite and Ammonite raiders against him. He sent them to destroy Judah, in accordance with the word of the LORD proclaimed by his servants the prophets. Surely these things happened to Judah*

*according to the LORD's command, in order to remove them from his presence because of the sins of Manasseh and all he had done, **including the shedding of innocent blood. For he had filled Jerusalem with innocent blood, and the LORD was not willing to forgive.***

God will smite the rebellious for sin and God will spare the repentant in His mercy. After all, what is mercy if there is no judgment? The example in Ezekiel 9 shows that sighing and crying for the sins of the people was a prerequisite for receiving the merciful mark on the forehead. It is the lamenting and grieving over innocent bloodshed, idol worship, and detestable sinfulness that will precede the posting of a mark on our brow. It is true heart-wrenching grief that flows from a righteous character. It is not something a person can feign, and those who try are spiritual goats, hardened and in desperate need of repentance and grace.

Are you sighing and crying today? If Ezekiel's vision were literally fulfilled in America today, would the mark be placed on your head?

The innocent blood of over 41,600,000 babies has defiled America. The false god, Baal, is alive and well; the idol, Ashtoreth, invades the television screen, and women weep for Tammuz in every abortion clinic in the country.

It could be said that, "America has been filled with bloodshed, but will the Lord pardon?" It remains to be seen. Certainly the Church in America is not weeping over the sins committed within her walls. If the Christian Church would weep, the torrents of tears would wash through the land like a mighty cleansing flood. Instead, we see a parched and polluted land wanting for rain to rinse away the accumulated contamination of bloodguilt.[1] It is a warning to today's Christians that the walls of the temple did not keep out the axe-wielding angels in Ezekiel's time, and neither will the walls of our fellowships and churches today.

Many people say they are pro-life and claim to be against abortion but in reality they conform to the old pro-abortion bumper sticker theology: "Against abortion? Don't have one!" They would never bother to cross a street to save an innocent child from the hands of the hired killer lurking at the local Planned Parenthood facility. They cannot even bring themselves to admit that murder is taking place on that street, much less cross it.

In Ezekiel's day many people were called "Israel, the Chosen People," but few passed the test of sighing and crying. Today, many say they are Christians, but few could actually qualify to bear the mark of God upon their heads if the axe-wielding angels were to come through the land. Just as the slaughter in judgment began in the sanctuary of God (Ezekiel 9:6), so Peter, quoting Ezekiel, declares that judgment must begin in the House of God. *"For it is time for judgment to begin with the family of God; and if it begins with us, what will the outcome be for those who do not obey the gospel of God?"* (1 Peter 4:17). It is past time for the Church to get her house in order when it comes to the matter of innocent blood.

What it means to be pro-life is not whether one supports Operation Rescue or a crisis pregnancy center. It is not being against partial-birth abortion or voting Republican. It is a way of life. People who are truly pro-life will conform

---

[1] The cover art created by Mitch Irion for this book was inspired by this concept.

to the character of Christ. They will have a broken heart over the atrocities that also grieve God. They will weep and mourn for the sins of the people and for the innocent whose blood is shed thereby. They will perceive the face of Christ in the hidden faces of these tiny children. They will not bow the knee before the false gods of sexual perversion, child-sacrifice, convenience, or "choice," neither will they turn a blind eye to the defenseless as they are unjustly murdered in their local communities. They will not cower in the winepress. They will speak for the voiceless, support the woman in need, work to effect change, and warn the wicked.

Over a million needlessly die each year!

ABORTION
God have mercy on us!

Operation Rescue West operates a fleet of Truth Trucks that travel across America bearing witness to the tragic consequences of abortion.

Photos by Troy Newman

One Dead One Wounded

ABORTION
God have mercy on us!

One of ORW's Truth Trucks sits in front of the United States Supreme Court in Washington, D.C., where abortion was decriminalized in 1973.

Part Four

The Road
to
Restoration

Rejoice, O Gentiles, with His people;
For He will avenge the blood of His servants,
And render vengeance to his adversaries;
He will provide atonement for
His land and His people.
Deuteronomy 32:43

Chapter 17

For he who avenges blood remembers; he does not ignore the cry of the afflicted.
Psalm 9:12

The Way Home

Bloodguilt. Over 41,600,000 lives testify against us individually, as a community, as a Church, and as a nation. Our complicity in the crime of murder is inescapable. It is clear what price needs to be paid for the shedding of innocent blood and equally clear that the price has not been paid either by civil justice, by His people's trust in Christ's innocent blood for payment on this score, or by God exacting justice through judgment. The voice of innocent blood cries out to God continually for vengeance. Knowing this, we can never again read the Scriptures without being reminded that we stand in danger of God's judgment for our culpability in the shedding of innocent blood.

When moms, dads, and abortionists are added together, well over 100,000,000 people bear personal bloodguilt for at least one abortion. The doctrine of community bloodguilt found in Scripture further implicates the entire nation. The perpetrators are far too numerous and the bloodguilt has spread too far. We deserve God's judgment.

In addition to our personal guilt in abortion, the United States government has abrogated its responsibility to properly deal with the blood-guilty. This responsibility rightly involves executing convicted murderers, including abortionists, for their crimes in order to expunge bloodguilt from the land and people. Instead, the act of abortion has been elevated to a "God-given right" and the abortionists canonized as saints. Consequently, the entire nation has the blood-red stain of the lives of the innocent upon its head.

In response to this massive bloodguilt, we must not take the road of Judas, the road of the Pharisees, or the road that the chief priests took when they were each confronted with this issue. Judas, overwhelmed with the enormity of his sin, hung himself. The Pharisees, realizing the abominable nature of sin against God, turned God's law into a checklist as if a perfect exterior was the same as a heart after God. The chief priests denied their bloodguilt, recognizing only a threat to their power base. They refused to admit wrongdoing or to take matters of the heart or law seriously. They would not let God rule by His Spirit in their life and ministry. The road of the Pharisees and the chief priests led to their condemnation in Matthew 23, then, a generation later in 70 AD, to the destruction and removal of all in which they had trusted.

We cannot look at the enormity of innocent blood and give up as those who have no hope. We also cannot reduce the solution to a few (or many) things to do on a checklist or treat it with denial since its reality would threaten all we are and have. All of those roads will lead to the destruction and removal of all you trust in and stand for.

Many of the stories and analogies discussed in this book have been from the Scriptures, the foundation for daily living. The Bible uses the lives of real people to instruct us on how we should conduct our affairs and ourselves. When we see the accounts of men and women like Pilate, Jonah, Jerub-Baal, Judas, Elijah, Cain, Paul, Jezebel, Peter, and all the others, we know that their experiences, good and bad, were recorded to show us how we must live. Through studying their exploits, we can learn to avoid their mistakes and imitate their brave deeds. We can discover from them the narrow path to follow and the broad trail to avoid. Even their misdeeds can help us to understand the injustice and wickedness in our own nation and in our own hearts. First Corinthians 10:11-12 declares, *"These things happened to them as examples and were written down as warnings for us, on whom the fulfillment of the ages has come. So if you think you are standing firm, be careful that you do not fall!"*

When we walk in obedience to Christ, learning from the Scriptural examples, God promises: *"After the suffering of his soul, he will see the light of life and be **satisfied**; by his knowledge My righteous servant will justify many, and He will bear their iniquities"* (Isaiah 53:11).

God wants your heart (Proverbs 23:26). With your heart in His care, your actions and life will be free to bring glory to God through submission and obedience to His Law, out of love for Him and your neighbor, including your pre-born neighbor.

There is a road we must travel to free ourselves, our families, our churches, and our nation from bloodguilt. The road is straight and narrow and few now seem to have the courage to follow its arduous path. The road of Judas and the Pharisees was wide and easy to traverse, but the steps toward restoration are more difficult. The path must be followed with commitment and perseverance for a lifetime.

There is no short cut and no tram to get us to the end of the road quickly. There is no satisfaction that if we do it all right our efforts will suffice. Once on the pathway to restoration, there can be no turning back. The trip will cost you all you own, possibly your very life.

In Matthew 16, Jesus promises to all who would follow Him something radically different from anything that anyone had ever heard.

> *From that time on Jesus began to explain to His disciples that He must go to Jerusalem and suffer many things at the hands of the elders, chief priests and teachers of the law, and that He must be killed and on the third day be raised to life. Peter took Him aside and began to rebuke Him. "Never, Lord!" he said. "This shall never happen to you!" Jesus turned and said to Peter, "Get behind me, Satan! You are a stumbling block to Me; you do not have in mind the things of God, but the things of men."*

> *Then Jesus said to his disciples, "If anyone would come after Me, he must deny himself and take up his cross and follow Me. For whoever wants to save his life will lose it, but whoever loses his life for me will find it. What good will it be for a man if he gains the whole world, yet forfeits his soul? Or what can a man give in exchange for his soul?* (Matthew 16: 21-26).

And again Jesus echoed this in John 12:24, *"I tell you the truth, unless a kernel of wheat falls to the ground and dies, it remains only a single seed. But if it dies, it produces many seeds."*

Does this sound difficult? To the world, it is impossible, but in Christ we know that God gives grace and strength to those who put their hand to the plow for His sake. Jesus promises, *"My yoke is easy and my burden is light"* (Matthew 11:30).

The fundamental issue is not whether will you join the pro-life cause, but whether you will join God and His vision to transform the earth, starting with the piece of the rock that is under your own feet. If God's Law has been written on your heart and His mark placed upon your forehead in living letters for the entire world to read, all who see you will know where you stand. Will you act on God's call as one does who is saved, or will you bury your talent as one does who is not a fit vessel for Christ's use?

Those who are unconvinced that abortion is wrong, unwilling to admit any responsibility, or refuse to lay down their lives for the cause of righteousness might as well not bother to read the following chapters. Those in that unrepentant state are unable to discern God's heart in this matter and will probably go to their grave blood-guilty, their souls corrupted with the innocent blood of murdered children. They can only look forward to the time when, at death, they will hear the innocent children howling their names in testimony against them, demanding vengeance. The Bible speaks clearly about the fate of those who embrace or excuse murder and sexual immorality.

> *But the cowardly* [those who are afraid to walk in obedience], *the unbelieving, the vile, the murderers* [including abortionists and those who support them directly or indirectly], *the*

sexually immoral [adherents to the Planned Parenthood philosophy], *those who practice magic arts, the idolaters* [those who place anything above obedience to Christ, including their reputations and material comforts] *and all liars—their place will be in the fiery lake of burning sulfur. This is the second death* (Revelation 21:8).

Those, however, who are willing to admit to the responsibility we all bear, are eager to be transformed by the renewing of their minds, and are willing to lose their lives for the cause of Christ, would do well to continue on with the following chapters that detail what the Bible states about the way home, the way of life that leads to restoration to a righteous King.

The road that we must ravel – the path of restoration – is taken directly from the Scriptures, but it can only be traveled by those whose hearts are changed. When followed by God's people, it purges families, as well as our churches and land, of the bloodguilt that now haunts our nation and us. The three-part plan is simplified into three "R"s: Repentance, Rebuke, and Rescue. Only through these acts, taken soberly and together from the heart, can we expect to be restored to the blessings of righteousness.

The three steps of restoration are steps that will lead the heart described by Matthew 5:3-8 back to *"one nation under God, indivisible, with liberty and justice **for all.**"*

Blessed are the poor in spirit, for theirs is the kingdom of heaven. Blessed are those who mourn, for they will be comforted. Blessed are the meek, for they will inherit the earth. Blessed are those who hunger and thirst for righteousness, for they will be filled. Blessed are the merciful, for they will be shown mercy. Blessed are the pure in heart, for they will see God (Matthew 5:3-8).

This is the road home. God saved you with a father's love and started you on a life-long journey of obedient service to Him. He accompanies you on the journey, upholding and preserving you with that same love, and He is waiting for you with a father's love at the end of that road. It is essential that you start your journey now.

Chapter 18

The Lord is near to those who have a broken heart, and saves such as have a contrite spirit.
Psalm 34:18

Repent

King David cried out to God for forgiveness in Psalm 51:14, *"Deliver me from the guilt of bloodshed, O God, The God of my salvation."* David was responsible for murdering Uriah the Hittite in order to cover for his adultery with Uriah's wife, Bathsheba. The Prophet Nathan revealed David's bloodguilt through a prophetic parable that caused David to admit responsibility for his sin and return, once again, to God in the great prayer of repentance recorded as Psalm 51.

America is in much the same spiritual condition as King David before his famous confession. The sexual revolution has led to the murder of millions of innocent children in a vain effort to cover sexual indiscretions. America must follow King David's example of repentance. A repentant and contrite heart was the first step in David's restoration. In like manner, we must, by God's grace, recognize our sin and turn from it, then cry out to God in humility for deliverance from the guilt of bloodshed.

The hope for the cleansing of America's soil lies in a very familiar verse. Second Chronicles 7:14 is well known to most evangelicals but the precise words of the verse are rarely regarded and analyzed. Let us look carefully at those important words.

> **"If my people, who are called by my name, will humble themselves and pray and seek my face and turn from their wicked ways, then will I hear from heaven and will forgive their sin and will heal their land."**

The first thing we must do is to divest ourselves of the notion that this promise is unconditional. Second Chronicles 7:14 is an "if-then" verse. In the first section of the passage, certain conditions must be met before the second section of the verse, containing the promises of God, can be realized. Unfortunately, Christians who like to use this verse, often skip the all-important series of actions and focus only on the prayer mandate in the verse. Look closely at the full list of requirements mentioned in the passage.

If my people who are called by my name. This phrase defines who must perform the conditional acts before God. The Lord is placing the requirements upon His own people, those who are called by the name of Jesus the Christ. The responsibility for the future of America rests squarely on the shoulders of Christians.

Will humble themselves. The people of Nineveh humbled themselves before the Lord after hearing Jonah preach God's message of repentance. Even the kings of the city humbled themselves with sackcloth and ashes. Because of this act of contrition, God turned away His wrath and spared the city from destruction.

Perhaps the best example of humility is found in the gospel account of Jesus' life. Although fully God and deserving of all honor, He placed Himself in the lowly position of a servant and washed the feet of His followers as an example for His people to follow.

The kind of humility that satisfies the standard of this verse is not the kind of false humility that the Pharisees liked to display, making a show of their fasting, prayers, and charitable acts. Jesus spoke at length against the religious leaders of His day that were not unlike many of our leaders.

> Then Jesus said to the crowds and to his disciples: "The teachers of the law and the Pharisees sit in Moses' seat. **So you must obey them and do everything they tell you. But do not do what they do, for they do not practice what they preach.** They tie up heavy loads and put them on men's shoulders, but they themselves are not willing to lift a finger to move them. **Everything they do is done for men to see:** They make their phylacteries wide and the tassels on their garments long; **they love the place of honor at banquets and the most important seats** in the synagogues; they love to be greeted in the marketplaces and to have men call them `Rabbi.' But you are not to be called `Rabbi,' for you have only one Master and you are all brothers. And do not call anyone on earth `father,' for you have one Father, and he is in heaven. Nor are you to be called `teacher,' for you have one Teacher, the Christ. **The greatest among you will be your servant.** <u>**For whoever exalts himself will be humbled, and whoever**</u>

humbles himself will be exalted" (Matthew 23:1-12).

True humility for the Christian begins when he gets on his knees.   He must prostrate himself with an attitude of true repentance and meekness before the God he has offended, seeking God's grace to become the servant that God will use for His work.   The meek, who humbly submit themselves to the harness of God, will inherit the earth.

And pray. Through Christ's work on the cross that tore the temple veil from top to bottom, those who have been redeemed by the shed blood of Jesus can have access to God through prayer. With the correct humble attitude, the Christian can begin to speak to God, and make his requests.

> *Let us therefore come boldly to the throne of grace, that we may obtain mercy and find grace to help in time of need* (Hebrews 4: 16).

Disobedient hearts, however, will not be heard unless theirs is first the prayer of repentance.

> *If anyone turns a deaf ear to the law, even his prayers are detestable* (Proverbs 28:9).

The proper attitude before God is most important. Consider what the Lord said in Isaiah 1:15-17, *"When you spread out your hands in prayer, I will hide my eyes from you; even if you offer many prayers, I will not listen. Your hands are full of blood; wash and make yourselves clean. Take your evil deeds out of my sight! Stop doing wrong, learn to do right! Seek justice, rebuke the oppressor, defend the fatherless, plead the case of the widow."* God would not listen to the prayers of the people Isaiah was speaking to since they were willful, proud, unrepentant, and guilty of shedding innocent blood.

Seek My face. The humbled, praying Christian must diligently seek the face of the Lord. In order to search for God, one needs only to look as far as His written Word. God has revealed Himself and His decrees in the Holy Bible. Prayer must conform to the will of God as expressed in the Holy Scriptures. Effective prayer, in Jesus' Name, will be fervent prayer in agreement with the revealed will of God and His commandments, such as *"Do not murder."*

And turn from their wicked ways. Repentance is required before restoration can begin. Repentance not only means sorrow, but includes turning away from that for which we are sorrowful. It means that if there was an opportunity to do it all over again, we would not disobey God. Jesus said in John 14:15, "If you love me keep my commandments." Christians must wholeheartedly and enthusiastically turn from child killing to child-protection and nurture. We will not only try to make it illegal, but we will be there to minister to every woman and threatened child. The fruits of repentance for our every involvement in the innocent bloodshed will result in caring for our pre-born neighbor. Our eyes will be open to see what we refused to see, to love what we once were indifferent about, to protect what we once killed, to submit to God's Law, which we before disobeyed. By God's grace, the humbled, praying, and repentant Christian, applying God's Word to his actions, will wholly transform his lifestyle in conformation to God's revealed Word.

God uses the second part of the passage to detail His promises for those who comply with the first part of 2 Chronicles 7:14. Look closer at His promises.

Then I will hear from heaven. Many arrogant twenty-first century Christians wrongly believe that God must always heed their prayers regardless of their disobedient lives. They think God is sitting around heaven, like a jolly Santa Claus, just waiting to fill their Christmas wish lists masquerading as prayers, which they half-heartedly belch out as they fall into bed at night. Others may think they can demand some action from God as if commanding a genie in a bottle. *"You ask and do not receive, because you ask amiss, that you may spend it on your pleasures,"* (James 4:3). Yet others simply despair of it all, believing an answer to their prayer is like the dream of freedom to a man on death row.

The prayers of today's Christians would do better to begin with asking for forgiveness and mercy. *"If I regard iniquity in my heart, the Lord will not hear"* (Psalm 66:18). On the other hand, the man with a clear heart and pure motives, asking according to God's will in faith, can expect God to hear. *"The effective, fervent prayer of a righteous man avails much"* (James 5:16).

And forgive their sin. After coming into compliance with the conditional requirements in the first part of the verse, the Lord God of Creation promises to forgive the sins of His people. The bloodguilt will be assuaged. The black stain of murder will be remembered no more and the sin of child-sacrifice will be removed from God as far as the East is from the West. Joel 3:21 speaks to this forgiveness for those who walk in repentance and righteousness: "Their bloodguilt, which I have not pardoned, I will pardon." This is the Good News. This is the Gospel of Christ! As the old hymn says, "Jesus paid it all, all to Him I owe… He washed me white as snow!" Oh, how fragrant is the bouquet of forgiveness! How precious and unique is the shed blood of our Lord, Who is able to pardon our transgressions and forget our offenses!

> *For he has rescued us from the dominion of*
> *darkness and brought us into the kingdom of*
> *the Son he loves, in whom we have redemption,*
> *the forgiveness of sins* (Colossians 1:13-14).

And will heal their land. Christ's atonement is able to achieve the impossible. Through it, the nation, polluted with the bloodshed of millions of innocent babies, will be purified. The land will cease to vomit out its inhabitants and will, instead, bring forth abundant fruit in its season to sustain and bless the inhabitants. God will purify the cities and the countryside so that the soil will no longer hold the curse of innocent blood. Like the driving rain that washed Mt. Carmel after the prophets of Baal were righteously executed, the land will cease to be defiled.

No more will children murder each other in school shootings. Illicit drugs and sexual perversion, rites performed to a modern day version of the demon idols Baal and Ashtoreth, will be expunged from our country. God will release America from the grip of judgment, as the personal and community bloodguilt is cleansed. The cries of vengeance of the slain will cease, for God's people will have appeased their cry for justice through obedience and faith in the One whose blood speaks a better word than that of Abel. God will accomplish His promised healing and restoration only to the nation of those who are transformed by humble obedience.[1]

Proverbs 28:13 declares, *"He who conceals his sins does not prosper, but whoever confesses and renounces them*

---

[1] Recommended reading: *Paradise Restored* by David Chilton, Dominion Press, 1999

finds mercy." In essence, 2 Chronicles 7:14 is a conditional promise of mercy.

America today is a nation hiding her sin. She has denied this sin by brazenly decriminalizing it in Roe vs. Wade. She covers for it by renaming it "choice." She encourages it through state and federal funding. She defends it by arresting and prosecuting those who would stand against it. She shakes her finger at nations like China and Iraq for "human rights abuses" and all the while her skirts are full of blood. America stands defiant in the face of warnings of God's impending judgment, but in reality she is in desperate need of mercy. Oh, that the kindhearted hand of God would reach down from heaven in mercy upon a nation that has confessed and renounced child-killing! For the dreadful sin of abortion we must all cry aloud: God have mercy on us!

When will Ezekiel's description of a people who "sigh and cry" describe us?

Let the reader mourn for the babies, whose tender lives have been snuffed out by the contract killers. Beg God to place a saving mark upon your forehead to distinguish you from the heathen in the land and pray to be saved from the axe-wielding angels of death who will surely come to smite our nation, beginning in our churches. Draw a circle on the ground and stand in the middle of it. Repentance begins in that circle; it starts with you.

Chapter 19

The words of the wicked lie in wait for blood, but the speech of the upright rescues them.
Proverbs 12:6

Rebuke

Jesus commissioned every believer, from the time of the Apostles on, to *"Go and make disciples of all nations, baptizing them in the name of the Father and of the Son and of the Holy Spirit, and teaching them to obey everything I have commanded you..."* (Matthew 28: 19-20). Thus, the Apostle Paul was following Christ's words precisely when he went out street preaching. Paul toured the synagogues and market places. He preached on street corners and in amphitheaters. Every step of the way, he lectured on Christ and the Law of God. He preached the Gospel, he warned evildoers, and he rebuked the wicked. Nearing the end of his earthly life and ministry, Paul declared himself to be innocent of the blood of all men.

> But when the Jews opposed Paul and became abusive, he shook out his clothes in protest and said to them, **"Your blood be on your own heads***! I am clear of my responsibility. From now on I will go to the Gentiles* (Acts 18:6).

> *Therefore, I declare to you today that **I am innocent of the blood of all men**. For I have*

not hesitated to proclaim to you the whole will of God (Acts 20:26-27).

How could Paul claim to be guiltless of innocent blood? It was, after all, he who consented to having Deacon Stephen stoned to death. However, Paul was not speaking concerning the murder of anyone. He was talking about a *spiritual bloodguilt.*

The passages above refer to certain verses recorded in Ezekiel chapters 3 and 33 that teach the "watchman on the wall" principle. This doctrine is important enough for the Lord to have covered it twice in the book of Ezekiel, as well as in other scattered verses in various parts of the Word. It is essential for followers of Christ to understand why Paul declared his innocence in Acts. The following passages help explain Paul's declaration.

At the end of seven days the word of the LORD came to me: "Son of man, I have made you a watchman for the house of Israel; so hear the word I speak and give them warning from me.

"When I say to a wicked man, 'You will surely die,' and you do not warn him or speak out to dissuade him from his evil ways in order to save his life, that wicked man will die for his sin, and I will hold you accountable for his blood.

"But if you do warn the wicked man and he does not turn from his wickedness or from his evil ways, he will die for his sin; but you will have saved yourself.

*"Again, when a righteous man turns from his
righteousness and does evil, and I put a
stumbling block before him, he will die. Since
you did not warn him, he will die for his sin.
The righteous things he did will not be
remembered, and I will hold you accountable
for his blood.*

*"But if you do warn the righteous man not to
sin and he does not sin, he will surely live
because he took warning, and you will have
saved yourself"* (Ezekiel 3:16-20).

*The word of the LORD came to me: "Son of
man, speak to your countrymen and say to
them: `When I bring the sword against a land,
and the people of the land choose one of their
men and make him their watchman, and he
sees the sword coming against the land and
blows the trumpet to warn the people, then if
anyone hears the trumpet but does not take
warning and the sword comes and takes his
life, his blood will be on his own head. Since
he heard the sound of the trumpet but did not
take warning, his blood will be on his own head.
If he had taken warning, he would have saved
himself. But if the watchman sees the sword
coming and does not blow the trumpet to warn
the people and the sword comes and takes the
life of one of them, that man will be taken away
because of his sin, but I will hold the watchman
accountable for his blood'"* (Ezekiel 33:1-6).

Paul shook out his clothes and declared himself clear
of his responsibility because he had not failed to preach the

whole counsel of God, taking diligence to warn the wicked of their wrongdoing and rebuke the oppressors as they floundered in their sin. The Apostle clearly said it was the preaching of the whole Word of God that made him innocent of the blood of all mankind. Paul was ready, in season and out of season, to preach, seeing to it that he rebuked, exhorted and admonished all men. A man willing to be a watchman must be willing to confront sin, however unpopular that may be.

One can even imagine Paul, as he worked at sewing tents, admonishing his co-workers for stealing tent cloth. (*"Let him that stole steal no more"* Ephesians 4:28.) It would not have been out of character for Paul to chide the sellers in the local marketplace for cheating their customers. Paul might have even confronted the prostitutes and their male companions while preaching forgiveness and deliverance in Christ. (*"Avoid every kind of evil"* 1 Thessalonians 5:22.) In order for Paul to boldly claim his innocence in light of the Ezekiel verses, Paul must have been a very diligent man.

Paul wrote, *"Therefore the law was our tutor, to bring us to Christ, that we might be justified by faith"* (Galatians 3:24, NKJV). Paul knew that when he rebuked a man for violating the law of God, he was in fact showing that man his sin so he could understand his need for salvation, and have the opportunity to turn to Christ. At the end of Paul's life, he told Timothy that he had been a good watchman, faithfully discharging his duties to warn the sinners in their way, (2 Timothy 4:6-8). If Paul were living today, we would probably find him at the local abortion mill warning the moms and dads entering the front door, offering them help and a better way in Christ, but also proclaiming a harsh word for the baby-killers leaving by the back door. Paul declared he was innocent of all men's blood because he successfully rebuked them as a faithful watchman.

Christians today must also be watchmen who, in humility and love, are ever vigilant to confront and warn those who commit wrongdoing. Christians must also warn society against the dangers of sin. Whether it be abortionists or congressmen, pastors or laymen, rich or poor, the mighty law of God will judge all men, everywhere, at all times. Good watchmen will warn and reprimand the workers of iniquity and in doing so will save their own lives. This is because he who is absolved of guilt and understands God's law can warn others from his heart as one who knows his own sin and God's grace. He has removed the log from his own eye and can clearly see to take the mote of sin out of his neighbor's eye (Matthew 7:1-5). However, he who is not absolved of sin understands neither God's law nor the gathering clouds of God's judgment. He does not warn others in a way that brings life, but rather excuses their wicked deeds, and in so doing, unwittingly shares in them. He ignores the fact that the wages of sin is death. Simply put: the saved rebuke the wicked, while those who keep their mouth shut proclaim their damnation.

The work of a watchman will be hard, thankless work. Matthew Henry's commentary on Ezekiel 3 says, "Such a dilemma are the church's watchmen in; men will curse them if they be faithful, and God will curse them if they be false." Do not look for all men to show appreciation for the rebuke. Rather, be on guard, for the good watchmen could end up like Paul who was beaten, whipped, and flogged. However, the joy in seeing lives change for the better as a result of the warning makes the toil worth every pain. One can also take heart in knowing that God sees and will reward every man according to his work.

It is unfortunate that pro-lifers can hardly go on the street to speak on behalf of the pre-born without a professing

Christian stopping to tell them that what they are doing is wrong. It usually starts something like this, "I'm a Christian and I'm pro-life but what you people are doing is not loving."

Proverbs 27:5 reminds believers that, *"Open rebuke is better than hidden love."* Open rebuke to a woman scheduled to kill her baby at the abortion clinic door sometimes results in a change of heart concerning the shedding of innocent blood. This rebuke is really an open act of love. Christians who carefully conceal their supposed love for the abortion-minded woman by not reaching out to her in her time of need are practically placing their stamp of approval on the murderous act. In reality, they prove by their inaction that they care little for the dead child or the long-term consequences that the aborting woman will now have to deal with.

Love for another does little good if that love will not act, (I Corinthians 13). The truly loving thing to do when one sees another in sin is to confront him concerning his error lest he continue on a path that will cause harm to him or others.

Rebuke truly has life-saving value. Rebuking evildoers can cause them to repent. Preaching the whole counsel of God can bring spiritual rebirth. Counseling women as they are about to enter the death camps to commit murder can spare babies' lives. *"The words of the wicked lie in wait for blood, but the speech of the upright rescues them"* (Proverbs 12:6).

The mouth is a very powerful tool. James compares the tongue to a tiny spark that ignites a mighty forest fire or a small rudder on a large ship able to navigate the vessel (James 3). The tongue can be a powerful implement to bring sinners to salvation and deter the evil from their destructive path.

Christians are often quick to appeal to grace but slow to seek justice. There must be an equal balance of the two. The Bible says, "***Righteousness*** *and* ***justice*** *are the foundation of His throne"* (Psalm 97:2). **The foundations of the throne of God!** Christians must never forget to preach the law and rebuke the oppressors for their sins. In doing so, they will not only give the evildoer an opportunity to repent, but will save themselves from the consequences of neglecting their duty as watchmen.

In summary: following repentance from our complacency and indifference toward the fate of pre-born children and their mothers, rebuke is a basic step in the restoration of the American culture to a safe haven for our precious posterity.

Chapter 20

Rescue those being led away to death;
hold back those staggering toward slaughter. If you say,
"But we knew nothing about this,"
does not he who weighs the heart perceive it?
Does not he who guards your life know it? Will he not
repay each person according to what he has done?
Proverbs 24:11-12

Rescue

Scott was a mild man who found a church home at West Hills Christian Fellowship. He was an usher at church and was well liked by everyone in the congregation. When the Pastor and church decided to begin an active pro-life ministry, Scott jumped in with both feet. He could be seen regularly at the local death center holding a sign. Once after encountering a demonstration by the People for the Ethical Treatment of Animals (PETA), Scott quipped, "I am pro-choice when it comes to eating meat." As they further debated, the PETA folks, who were in favor of abortion, were confounded by Scott's keen insight on the subject.

Although Scott was a peace-loving man, he could not be mistaken for a coward. While at home with his sister and nephews one day, his sister's deranged ex-husband charged into the home wielding a knife. Scott did not hesitate. Unarmed, Scott placed himself between the assailant and his sister's family. He was repeatedly stabbed in the neck, chest, face, and eyes while he fought for the lives of his family. The brutal attack lasted only a few moments before Scott collapsed, hemorrhaging from multiple stab wounds. However, Scott was able to buy enough time for his sister to quickly dial 911. Those precious moments of time were purchased with Scott's life but it was just enough time to save the lives of his defenseless sister and her children. Scott selflessly intervened to stop the shedding of innocent blood, at the cost of his own life.

Scott lived and died a Rescuer. In his life he rescued children from execution at abortion mills. He did no less in his death. Jesus once said, *"Greater love has no one than this, that he lay down his life for his friends"* (John 15:13). Scott, the Rescuer, lived and died a hero. More importantly, his life and death are a testimony to the way that all of us should act every day.

The Lord demands that we should *"Rescue those being led away to death; hold back those staggering toward slaughter"* (Proverbs 24:11).

The Lord requires that we *"Defend the cause of the weak and fatherless; maintain the rights of the poor and oppressed. Rescue the weak and needy; deliver them from the hand of the wicked"* (Psalm 82:3-4).

James defined true homage toward the Savior when he wrote, *"Religion that God our Father accepts as pure and faultless is this: to look after orphans and widows in their distress and to keep oneself from being polluted by the world"* (James 1:27).

Scott learned to defend the innocent through the preaching ministry of West Hills Christian Fellowship. He simply lived out the Word of God that was reinforced in his life through daily Bible readings. Isaiah 1 records a rebuke to those who pretended to be God's people and lists a number of things that true believers should do. *"Wash yourselves, make yourselves clean; put away the evil of your doings from before My eyes. Cease to do evil, learn to do good; seek justice, rebuke the oppressor, defend the fatherless, plead the cause of the poor and needy."* It could be said of Scott that he had learned to do right. Scott sought justice, he rebuked the oppressor, he defended the fatherless, and he pleaded for the widow. Scott was a rescuer through and through.

Rescue, contrary to popular perceptions, is more than an act of sitting in front of the door leading to an abortionist's death chamber: it is a way of life. We rescue when we use our mouths to speak up for the oppressed. We rescue when we fall on our faces before God and weep over the innocent blood spilled in our land. We rescue when we rebuke the baby killers and their minions. We rescue when we lay down our lives for the defenseless pre-born babies who go to their deaths every day. This is the pure and undefiled religion of visiting the widows and orphans in their desperate struggle for life.

The churches of our day are, like Gideon, threshing wheat in a winepress, as the evil in our land and in our churches increase. The truly repentant Christian will show the fruits of his changed heart by abhorring acts like those of the Levite and the Priest in the parable of the Good Samaritan. Desiring instead obedience to his Master, he will no longer allow himself to pass by on the other side when faced with the needy. He will start acting like the Good Samaritan. Jesus said that the man who was righteous and followed God's decrees was the man who picked up the dying man from the road and aided in his recovery, all the while bearing the full weight and cost of his rescue effort. Is this not what the Lord means when He tells us to bear each other's burdens and to love our neighbor as we love ourselves?

Rescue is action that flows from a transformed heart. Scott saw a need and fought hard for the lives of his family members. He did not need to go pray and fast before deciding if it was God's will that he stand between the murderer's knife and his innocent family. *"Is not this the kind of fasting I have chosen: to loose the chains of injustice and untie the cords of the yoke, to set the oppressed free and break every yoke?"* (Isaiah 58:6). This was instead the "fast" that he observed as each knife jab plunged into his body.

Scott did not need to stop and read his Bible to find the perfect verse to tell him that he needed to face the deadly wounds. He became a living epistle as he bled there on the floor. Scott did not delay, hoping someone else would fight for him, and neither did he call his pastor to get permission. No, Scott dove in and rescued. For him, it was a way of life and a way of death. Ultimately it is the way of the cross. *"Whoever tries to keep his life will lose it, and whoever loses his life will preserve it"* (Luke 17:33).

As Christians, we must be ever ready to sacrifice our own lives for others. When we signed our lives over to Christ on the day of our salvation, few of us understood the full implications of the fine print on the contract. It read in part, "Must be ready to esteem others higher than yourselves. Must be willing to lay down your life for others." This is what Jesus meant when he said, *"Love your neighbor as yourself."*

Does this sound strange? To a non-Christian it will,

but God-fearing men and women understand that the Christian life will appear strange to the people of this world. In order for one to live, he must first die. In order for one to be first, he must be the last. If someone wants to become great in the Kingdom of God, he must first become the servant of all. In order to become full, he must become empty. In order to gain his life, he must first lose it. This is the Christian way.

For believers, rescue is the marching order of the day. Jesus came with the ultimate rescue operation to save mankind from the weight of its sin. His victory over death and sin is fully manifest in our own lives only when we reflect His nature in our actions, that is, when we rescue.

The mission field is right in your hometown and the arena for service is within your own community's gates where abortion-minded moms walk our streets and sit in our church pews. We must reach out to the women and men who believe there is no other choice than to shed the innocent blood of their own precious babies. Although the First Amendment of the U.S. Constitution protects our rights to publicly speak out and distribute literature, it may not always be so. It may never be required, but we must be willing to sacrifice our jobs, homes, and the prospect of a so-called normal life for the cause of Christ and to rescue the babies slated for death.

In a nation whose laws promote abortion on demand (child-sacrifice), the price of rescue has often been high. Even so, very few have paid the price that Scott paid. Jail time, fines, and lawsuits await many a rescuer, but that price is small compared to the saints who have gone before us.

Remember those earlier days after you had received the light, when you stood your ground in a great contest in the face of suffering.

Sometimes you were publicly exposed to insult and persecution; at other times you stood side by side with those who were so treated. You sympathized with those in prison and joyfully accepted the confiscation of your property, because you knew that you yourselves had better and lasting possessions. So do not throw away your confidence; it will be richly rewarded. You need to persevere so that when you have done the will of God, you will receive what He has promised. For in just a very little while, "He who is coming will come and will not delay. But my righteous one will live by faith. And if he shrinks back, I will not be pleased with him." But we are not of those who shrink back and are destroyed, but of those who believe and are saved (Hebrews 10:32-39).

We must run this race to win. As Christians, we must not shrink back in the face of adversity, but should rather trust God to preserve and empower His people who walk in obedience. The Scriptures speak clearly. *"Greater is He who is in me than he who is in the world"* (1 John 4:4). *"Resist the devil and he will flee from you"* (James 4:7). These are covenantal promises from the One who never breaks His Word.

There are those who have carefully worked out their excuses in life so that protecting their material possessions, their family's comfort, their church routines, or the status quo of the world can be well argued from selected Scriptures. They raise their children thoroughly insulated from understanding their duty to engage the wicked culture in battle, only to discover that in doing so they have taught their children that Christ gives no power to overcome the world. Their only power is to build a self-serving wall that the world is always threatening to breach. After a life of building that wall, they find that they have no energy left to reach a dying world, to take up their cross, to spend and be spent for the kingdom, or to see the gates of hell come down. Our children must be taught through parental example that faith will overcome fear and grant strength to rescue a lost world for Christ. This is the lesson our children must see if we are to pass on a faith that has any relevance in their lives or in the world.

> *But seek first his kingdom and his righteousness, and all these things will be given to you as well* (Matthew 6:33).

Do not wait until you are lying upon your deathbed to examine your life's accomplishments. Take a moment now to ponder the time God has given you here on earth and review your life's work. What did you do with the days of your youth? What did you do with the gifts the Lord has provided to you? Were you a good steward of the your time, energy, resources, and the breath in your lungs? In the end, all that matters in life is what we were able to do for others in obedience to God's Word.

Rescue today and rescue often. Make your life count for God. You will not live to regret the sacrifice or the impact your life will have on the world around you. Your presence at an abortion clinic as a sidewalk counselor or a prayer warrior may save a mother from committing murder and a child from being destroyed. At the very least, you will be a faithful witness for Christ.

The story has often been told of a grandfather and

his four-year-old grandson. The two of them were walking on a beach the day after a great storm had blown through. The seashore was littered with thousands upon thousands of the little starfish that had been blown ashore by the high seas. As the two meandered down the sandy beach, the young boy would occasionally pick a starfish up and toss it back into the ocean. The boy's grandfather lovingly asked the child, "Why bother throwing them back? There are so many dying it hardly makes a difference." The boy looked with resolve at his grandpa, and then fixed his eyes upon the starfish he gripped in his hand. "It makes a difference to this one!" he replied as he pitched the little creature back into the water.

Day after day, pre-born boys and girls "wash up on the shore" of the death camps of the nation's abortion centers, driven, not by the tide, but by the pro-abortion culture. Acting upon the words of our Savior you can be their rescuer. You can make a difference in the lives of the pre-born, one at a time, as you stand in their defense, obeying the Biblical mandates to repent, rebuke, and rescue. May you be able to answer the questions about your life's work, having faithfully discharged your full duty to God, with the same pride and dignity of a military veteran recounting his faithful service to his beloved country.

At Scott's memorial service many from the community praised him for his selfless act of rescuing his family members from death. Although few of us will be called to expend our "last full measure of devotion" as did Scott, we all can follow his heroic example of obedient sacrifice by setting aside our personal comforts in order to rescue our pre-born neighbors.

And Jesus said, *"Go and do likewise!"*

Chapter 22

Therefore as surely as I live, declares the Sovereign LORD, I will give you over to bloodshed and it will pursue you. Since you did not hate bloodshed, bloodshed will pursue you.
Ezekiel 35:6

The Three-Legged Chair

The Yates family lived in a modest home nestled in a suburban neighborhood of Houston, Texas. "Nice folks" was a term used by many in the community to describe the growing family. Mary was the fifth child and the only girl in a family of brothers. Noah was 7, John, 5, Paul, 3, and little Luke was 2. At six months, Mary was her daddy's little princess. The children loved to spend the summer days swimming in a neighbor's pool. By all outward appearances, the family was happy, content, and well liked.

Yet one afternoon Andrea Yates systematically took each of her five babies and drowned them in the family bathtub. As Mrs. Yates carried Mary's lifeless little body from the bathroom, Noah sensed that something was wrong. He inquired of his Mommy about his little sister. Andrea simply placed the little girl in her bed next to Noah's three dead brothers then grasped for the oldest of the boys. Escaping her grip, Noah ran through the house in terror. The arms that once cuddled him, the tender hands that once spoon-fed him were now murdering him. Once Noah had been caught and killed, Andrea called her husband and calmly asked him to come home. Mrs. Yates was found guilty of murdering the three oldest of her children. Instead of receiving the death penalty, she was sentenced to life in prison, and will be eligible for parole in forty years. America will never be able to fully come to grips with this tragedy.

Just south of San Francisco is the small beach town of Menlo Park. It is just a mile north of Stanford University, but this quaint community is brimming with multi-million dollar homes. It boasts of estates owed by NFL superstars, computer chip capitalists, software moguls, and bioscience engineers. On the far side of the upscale community is a growing biotech industry. On any given day in the sterile labs of this biotech hub you will find molecular scientists working diligently to find cures for every human ailment or searching for unique ways to increase crop production.

However, at the Geron Corporation[1] you will find lab technicians peering into a petri dish containing five or more tiny human beings, babies the size of the period at the end of this sentence. Less than 100 cells big, these human embryos are at a point in life when their tiny cells can grow and divide into any cell in the human body. That is why Geron desperately wants these babies. Geron has patented a method of stripping the precious cells from the baby[2], killing him, and fusing the freshly harvested human cells with mice "feeder" cells, [3] which will cause them to grow into heart, liver, or skin cells.[4] The scientists take a living child and

[1] Geron Corporation web site: http://www.geron.com/.
[2] "Embryonic Stem Cell Patents" Geron Corporation, http://www.geron.com/.
[3] "Culturing Human Embryonic Stem Cells" Kimball's Biology Pages, http://users.rcn.com/jkimball.ma.ultranet/BiologyPages/H/HumanEScells.html.
[4] "Stem Cells: A Primer" National Institutes of Health, http://www.nih.gov/news/stemcell/primer.htm#6.

dismember him for the production of something more marketable. The scientific community lauds this embryonic stem cell research, and the future of this research is in the hands of Congress.

These seemingly different stories are at the root the same. Both accounts include the systematic murder of legally innocent children by a cruel outside force. Each of the two murderers was a natural caretaker. Mommies protect their own children and doctors nurture human life. But in both cases the natural order was perverted through a wicked betrayal. Mom murders her own babies and doctors destroy humanity they have vowed to protect. Put another way, it is a gross breech of justice.

Amos says, *"But let justice roll on like a river, righteousness like a never-failing stream!"* (Amos 5:24). When Christians seek justice for the pre-born children, God will begin to hear the prayers of the Church, as 2 Chronicles 7:14 teaches.

Justice for the shedding of innocent blood best occurs when the perpetrator is captured and convicted by a government whose laws reflect God's standards. Christians cannot hope to see the American legal system return to justice for the pre-born until the Church begins to exercise her responsibilities to do justice in the manner that God has prescribed for her. And what is preventing the church from doing this?

It is sinful fear that is holding back the churches from joining the battle. The fear of losing church buildings, fear of losing congregation members, fear of offending somebody, and fear of jail time will stop a person or church from completing the three acts of restoration. *"For God did not give us a spirit of timidity, but a spirit of power, of love and of self-discipline"* (2 Timothy 1:7). The cowardly churches and the people in them refuse to trust God, and take Him at His word when He said that He would be at their sides as they went into the world to act on His behalf (Matthew 28:20). Cowards are listed as the first group of sinners to *"have their part in the lake, which burns with fire and brimstone, which is the second death"* (Revelation 21:8, NKJV), and have no place among the faithful. The Bible admonishes us to put away fear and start seeking justice.

The work of justice lies in grace, mercy, and love. Grace is repenting, mercy is rebuking, and love is rescuing. Christians must practice all three of these principles before they can teach them to the nation. Only then will there be any hope for our laws to be amended to protect innocent babies and punish those who would brutally kill them, thereby purging the bloodguilt from the land and from its inhabitants.

Consider the example of a three-legged chair. A chair with three legs is stable; it does not tip. However, when one or two of the legs are removed, the destabilized chair will tip and the person on the seat will tumble downward.

The three principles of restoration: repentance, rebuking, and rescuing, are analogous to a three-legged chair. With all three principles in effect, restoration is the stable outcome. But remove one of the principles and stability is lost. Restoration thus collapses.

For example, repentance without rebuke and rescue is not true repentance at all. It will only produce crocodile tears, and a church unwilling to lift a finger to aid the pre-born babies for whom they are weeping. These are the churches that say they are praying for abortion, (whatever that means). Churches all over the nation fall into this category. It is easy to cry over the injustice of murder, but true justice demands action. Once sincere repentance had been made, the Christian will not only weep for the innocent, but will also commit to rebuking the enemies of life. He will seek ways to act out his convictions and physically rescue children from abortion.

Rebuke without repentance or rescue is hypocritical. It reflects that the plank has not been removed from the disciplinarian's eye. Humility and repentance come first. Only after dealing with the sin in his own life can that person legitimately obey the command to call sinners to repentance according to Ephesians 5:11, *"Have nothing to do with the unfruitful deeds of darkness, but rather expose them."*

The three concepts of repentance, rebuking the wicked, and rescuing the innocent are intertwined and interdependent. Repentance will inevitably lead to a change in life that will cause a person to rescue. A very important part of rescuing children is to rebuke the enemies who do the child killing. Pro-life ministries that leave out this important principle of restoration may have a nice work, but they will not bring our nation any closer to thwarting the impending judgment from God. We can help women in need, give them sonograms and diapers, but we must be willing to rebuke the child-killers, in addition to rendering meaningful assistance to women considering abortions. But all must be done with a repentant and humble heart.

James said that faith without works is dead (James 2:17), and Paul said that works without faith is dead (Ephesians 2:9-10). Remember the men of faith recorded in Hebrews 11? The faith of these men and women was proved by their works, their works proved their faith, and it all demonstrated that God was working in their life. Faith and consequent good works are inseparable; works are an evidence of faith while faith spawns good works. A repentant heart speaking out on behalf of the babies sentenced to die is an indication of faith.

> *He has showed you, O man, what is good. And what does the LORD require of you? To act justly and to love mercy and to walk humbly with your God* (Micah 6:8).

In order to walk humbly with God, we must do justice and love mercy. This is the Christian's life. In doing justice, the Christian will repent, rebuke, and rescue. In God's economy these three acts will not only prevent the shedding of innocent blood, but will also bring the final "R"s of revival and restoration to the land. The Lord gave us the tools to accomplish His work. He has promised that if we will use all of them we will bear fruit. We are to be like that tree in Psalm 1 planted by rivers of water, bearing fruit at the appropriate times.

> *For it is by grace you have been saved, through faith—and this not from yourselves, it is the gift of God—not by works, so that no one can boast. For we are God's workmanship, **created in Christ Jesus to do good works, which God prepared in advance for us to do*** (Ephesians 2:8-10).

In summary, the biblical principles of repenting, rebuking, and rescuing must be completed as a whole. One ministry cannot say to another, "Mine is to rescue and yours is to rebuke," just as a church cannot say to the missionary,

"Your work is to rescue lost souls and ours is to repent." All three concepts must be embraced and implemented before justice can be restored and the bloodguilt can be assuaged.

We must be ever mindful of the impending hand of judgment looming over our land because of the sin of innocent bloodshed through abortion. America is destined for ruin if the Christian Church does not obey the Bible and take an active stand against this abomination. Our nation, our churches, our brothers and sisters in Christ currently all labor under the curse of bloodguilt. Pre-born children are dying and it is your fault, it is my fault, it is our fault. The road to revival and restoration has been laid out clearly before us in unassailable biblical principles: repent in humility, rebuke in love, and rescue the innocent. Please, for the sake of those who will come after and reap the fruits of our actions, pick up your cross and follow Christ.

Appendices

Appendix A

An Open Letter to Pastors and Elders of the Christian Faith

Dear Pastor,

Every Christian pastor on earth has probably quoted Isaiah 1:18. Perhaps you have used it as a text for sermons and altar calls, or maybe your choir sings the lovely melody that accompanies this well-known verse:

> *Though your sins are like scarlet, they shall be as white as snow. Though they are red like crimson, they shall be as wool.*

Unfortunately, this celebrated verse is consistently quoted out of context. The sins of scarlet refer to the hands full of blood talked about in verse 15. It refers to the bloodguilt that comes upon a society where the shedding of innocent blood is tolerated, and that includes both the direct involvement in murder as well as the community bloodguilt shared by persons living in a land that permits it.

Today, as in Isaiah's day, blood flows freely through the sewers. The innocent blood shed within the borders of the United States is causing a crimson stain to come upon you, me, and every other inhabitant of our land. Over 41,6000 babies have been sacrificed on the modern-day version of the altar of Baal.

In Isaiah 1:14-15, we have a sobering revelation, especially for today's church in America:

> *Your New Moon festivals and your appointed feasts* [church services and assemblies] *my soul hates. They have become a burden to me; I am weary of bearing them. When you spread out your hands in prayer, I will hide my eyes from you; even if you offer many prayers, I will not listen. Your hands are full of blood;*

Being a pastor or elder is a high office and the responsibility you bear is very great. Part of your responsibility is to personally act in obedience to the One whom you have chosen to serve, then lead your flock in that same obedience. For our churches to enjoy the full blessings of obedience, you must come to grips with your involvement in child-murder and start down the road to restoration. If you have read this book, then you have been exposed to the Doctrine of Proximity and the Circle of Culpability as it relates to bloodguilt and you understand what God requires of you.

Though you may not realize it, your hands are defiled by the blood of aborted babies -- and so are mine. No one in America can claim to be blameless of the innocent blood of over 41,600,000 children. God is weary of bearing our prayers and He is hiding His eyes from our supplications. Furthermore, these children, though they are dead, yet they speak (Hebrews 11:4), crying out to God continuously for vengeance. The Bible assures us that He will avenge them.

That places you in a precarious situation. You bear personal responsibility in the abortion bloodbath. Your involvement is either direct or indirect. If you have participated in killing a baby by, for example, advising an abortion, then your sin is obvious. Even if you have only failed to speak out, failed to rebuke, failed to teach regularly on God's hatred of child-sacrifice; if you have failed to give Godly counsel to murders and murderesses, is equal to that of the knife-wielding abortionist, (Ezekiel 3, 33).

I give you the same challenge Elijah gave on Mount Carmel to a people tolerating child sacrifice in their land. *"How long will you waver between two opinions? If the LORD is God serve Him, but if Baal is god serve him"*... and be doomed!

After 41,600,000 dead babies, with no end in sight, I firmly believe God will no longer be satisfied with churches where sermons avoid the topic of child-sacrifice through abortion. According to precepts taught in Isaiah 1, God is not listening to the great praise music sung by those congregations. The prayers of their intercessors are falling on deaf ears. The preaching of the Word is hollow when it omits the tragic plight of the pre-born who are scheduled for death at our nearby abortion clinics.

Will you perceive the warning signs? Would you be shocked to learn that nearly 70% of all abortions occur on women who regularly attend the services of our churches? There are covenant children being dismembered on the altar of Baal regularly in your city and in mine! It is essential for you as a pastor to stand openly against this heinous crime.

Your obligation, like the Apostle Paul, is to preach the whole counsel of God and leave nothing unsaid. You must not fear to preach boldly against abortion. In fact, you should fear not to! It is your personal responsibility to rebuke the slayer, for in the image of God did God create man and Proverbs 6 reminds us that God hates the hands that shed the innocent blood of those created in His image.

Many pastors today like to reference as examples in the Christian faith such great men as Dietrich Bonhoeffer, a man who opposed Hitler's bloody regime and paid for it with his very life. Yet, most men of God today shame Bonhoeffer's memory by refusing to lift even a finger, let alone their voices, for the babies being slaughtered at the local abortion mill.

Today is the day and now is the time to act. Your congregation will follow if you will only lead. Will some of them leave? Perhaps, but those who stay will help you build a church that even the Gates of Hell cannot prevail against.

I charge you today to change the way you preach, revolutionize your method of evangelism, and transform your worship services into repentance sessions by focusing on the desires of God as revealed in Isaiah 1. Then show God your faith by your works of justice.

Only the Lord's mercy on a repentant church can cause the judgment for bloodguilt to be stayed. Our decisions concerning this issue could affect whether our children will enjoy the true liberty that can only be found in a nation who walks in repentance and obedience to God's precepts. Ultimately, if you do not follow God's restoration plan, you may be certain that the babies will continue to cry out to God for vengeance, and one of the names they will be calling wrath upon will be yours. God have mercy!

I urge you to follow the demands of Isaiah 1:16-17: *"Wash yourselves, make yourselves clean; put away the evil of your doings from before my eyes. Learn to do good; seek justice, rebuke the oppressor; defend the fatherless, plead for the widow."*

Only then can you rest assured that your crimson, blood-stained hands will be cleansed and become like pure white wool. Only in the full context can we lovingly and thankfully sing the chorus to Isaiah 1:18 and avoid the dreadful consequences mentioned in verse 20: *"But if you refuse and rebel, you shall be devoured by the sword'; for the mouth of the Lord has spoken."*

I pray with all my heart for you, the shepherd of your church, to lead the sheep into a real reformation and true revival, in Jesus name.

Speaking the truth in love,

Troy Newman
President, Operation Rescue West

PS I will respond personally to all correspondence and requests for further dialog.

Appendix B

Using Graphic Pictures

Christians displaying the deadly results of legal abortion on billboards and large hand-held signs are using an age-old tactic that has proven to be effective for generations. It is a tactic established in prayer, biblical mandate, and applicable historical examples.

Nearly every social cause in the last 150 years has used graphic imagery to change public opinion and to modify society's behavior. More importantly, God lays out several graphic presentations in His Word for the purposes of accomplishing the Lord's goal of saving creation from the weight of sin.

For example in Judges 19, we have the case of a Levite who cut his murdered wife into twelve pieces and sent the body parts throughout the land. The message communicated by her grisly remains was, "Consider, confer, and speak up!" The public outcry against this murder caused the nation of Israel to assemble "as one man" and end a terrible evil in Israel. Eventually this repentance sparked a nation-wide revival.

The detailed gory description of how a Jew would sacrifice a bull or lamb to atone for his sin is an area of the Scripture most people would rather not read but the importance is inescapable.

Every Christian is familiar with the graphic displays

of Jesus hanging naked, bloodied, and dead on a Roman cross. His broken body is the result of our sin; He suffered so that we might live. This vivid display alone brought many pagan South American Indians to a saving faith in Jesus Christ.

Moving to a historical reference, the abolition movement displayed the scars on runaway slaves at northern Church gatherings in an effort to persuade Christians to support the anti-slavery cause. Pictures of children working in harsh factory jobs led to the current child labor laws. The picture of the poor single mother working two jobs has been indelibly etched into our minds along with the words "Equal pay for equal work." The Vietnam War ended because of America's outrage; the pictures of body bags and bombed villages were moving enough to cause rioting in the streets. Need I mention the engrained images of suffering African Americans during the Civil Rights movement?

Animal "rights" activists used graphic displays of butchered, tusk-less elephants, their flesh rotting in the African sun, to spark a worldwide outcry against the bloody black-market ivory trade. The imagery of giant whales being stripped of their blubber on enormous whaling ships while the heroic activists placed themselves between the whaler's supercharged harpoon and the helpless next victim have set in motion world-wide prohibitions on whale harvesting.

Christian organizations like *World Vision* use the colored pictures of belly-swollen children to wrench our hearts into donating food and money toward their noble Christian action. *Voice of the Martyrs Magazine* routinely run ads depicting burned, mutilated, and scarred Christians, thereby highlighting the plight of the persecuted Church.

More recently, our nation entered into a war with

Yugoslavia over ethnic cleansing but only after being shocked into action from viewing the nightly news' explicit presentations of dead villagers. Don't forget the explicit anti-drinking and driving ads, anti-smoking, anti-gun commercials and so many more.

Yet, much of our country ignores the 41,600,000 (that's million) little boys and girls who have been dismembered in the ungodly act called abortion, a crime that screams injustice!

Today, most people, Christians included, have not a clue what happens in an abortion, or that child killing is **legal from conception to birth!** The pictures are crucial in revealing that truth. Showing society the bloodied remains of an aborted-child also rips away the façade of Planned Parenthood's respectability. Graphic signs have proven to save babies from abortion and turn hearts and minds towards life. Additionally, these public displays are a prophetic warning to a nation steeped in sin. Ephesians 5:11 tells us to, "*Have nothing to do with the unfruitful works of darkness but rather EXPOSE them.*"

Furthermore, God enlightens Ezekiel in chapter 22:2, "*Now, son of man, will you judge, will you judge the bloody city? YES, show her all her abominations!*" Clearly the Lord wanted Ezekiel to show (not tell) of all the abominations taking place in Israel. This verse in context reveals the bloodguilt of a nation steeped in child-sacrifice and sin.

Christians led by the Holy Spirit are following Biblical and historical examples in challenging the public with the sin of abortion. These signs are utterly horrific. They will cause an emotional reaction, especially for those who have chosen to kill their pre-born child. Children will see them. Christians will be viewed as "kooks and whackos" in the eyes of the world. It is not popular. But delivering a prophetic message to a sinful nation is rarely fashionable. Just ask John the Baptist after he admonished Herod on his sin of adultery. Hosea 9:7 declares, *"The prophet is a fool and the spiritual man is insane."*

Dare I pronounce a time for drastic action on behalf of the 3,300 babies torn to pieces every day? Dare I challenge Christians to put our respectability aside and sacrifice our reputations for the dying babies? Yes, and we will show the deadly results of abortion.

It is time to take our gloves off in this contest for life. It is time to shine the light of truth on the dark underworld of the abortion industry and the death merchants who operate with impunity in the hearts of our cities. As Americans grow comfortable with aborting babies on Main Street, the nation will be forced to view the result of that sin. With signs set up on street corners, billboards, and large trucks, the nation will be faced with the mutilated bodies of children that our silence and apathy helped to slay.

The torn faces of choice will cry out from the grave. Their pictures will be a solemn reminder that just around the corner another child is dying. **When you see them remember that the messenger is not the Christian holding the graphic picture but the infant whose bloodied face stares back at you.** What was done in secret will be brought to light!

May God forgive us for preferring the accolades of men above heeding His mandate to be a voice for the voiceless. And may He forgive us for being indifferent in an age that necessitates action. God forgive us — for our hands are covered in blood.

Appendix C

Face of War
By Troy Newman

On February 1, 1969, NBC photographer Eddie Adams happened upon two South Vietnamese soldiers escorting a prisoner through the streets of Saigon. The North Vietnamese were in the midst of their major Tet offensive, nearly overrunning the U.S. Embassy. The prisoner turned out to be a Viet Cong lieutenant responsible for the deaths of countless civilians.

Suddenly and out of nowhere General Nguyen Loan marched directly up to the prisoner. Drawing his revolver, the General placed the barrel on the Viet Cong's temple. Simultaneously, Eddie Adams raised his camera. The pistol fired and a split second later the shudder dropped on Eddie's equipment. The moment in time was trapped forever on the photographer's film.

The black and white still-photo illustrates the cold face of the executioner bracing the recoiling pistol along with the body of a living man being transformed into a corpse; still standing yet falling, still living yet already dead. The projectile penetrated one side of the victim's skull and visibly punched an exit hole on the other, his expression wincing from the percussion.

For right or wrong, the photograph was adopted by the American anti-war movement as a symbol of the excesses of war. The picture was viewed by millions of people and helped to sway the opinion of the nation against the war. Eddie Adams transported every viewer across time and space to a battlefield whose image so enraged the populace that the country was split in half. Never since the Civil War had the country been so divided.

A similar image has emerged today. It portrays an execution in a war nobody cares about. Unlike Viet Nam, politicians avoid the subject; newspapers and other media outlets have loathed covering it. Yet this picture is conveying viewers back in time and across space to a battlefield many have visited but few will admit is really there. This picture is a testimony to an undeclared war and proof of the excesses of our modern culture.

The picture, dated some ten years ago, was not taken on some foreign field of battle, but was snapped in Houston, Texas. The names of the participants are as unknown as the circumstances surrounding the untimely death. Even the photographer has chosen to remain anonymous. Yet the lifeless face of the victim tells the entire story. "Unwanted," "Inconvenient", or "Imperfect" could be the name placed upon the shattered remains. But results could no more be justified than the street shooting of the Viet Cong. The full-color picture displays the last gasp of a decapitated child grasped in an abortionist's cruel surgical tong.

This war is quietly raging in every large city in America. Even the combatants are unusual. Health Care professionals-turned-mercenaries are embarked upon a seek-and-destroy mission against those who cannot possibly defend themselves from such fierce aggression. This war looks more like genocide and the pre-born children are suffering heavy losses. The last thirty years have brought the death toll to nearly 45 million.

Just as a tourniquet can reduce an arterial hemorrhage, this one picture is turning the tide of the war. The medical personnel prosecuting this war are finally being questioned and the rules of engagement are in the process of redefinition. All because of one picture.

This photo has lined the streets across America and has been responsible for women turning away from the "field of battle," the abortion clinics. It has broken and changed the hearts of thousands. This limited display has had a huge impact on the small segment of the American people who have been exposed to it. Now, this one picture of one victim of America's silent, unpopular war needs to be displayed in the mass media market — no, it demands air-time!

Eddie Adam's graphic photo of that assassinated Viet Cong soldier helped to turn the conscience of America against a political, poorly waged war that was costing thousands of precious American lives. The picture of that unnamed baby can do the same in the Abortion War, yet those who should support such a change, the mainstream pro-life groups, resist the use of the most effective tool in the pro-life arsenal.

Why so much resistance to such a proven tactic? It is because abortion has touched nearly every life in one way or another. Nearly forty percent of all women will have had an abortion by the age of 40. Husbands, boyfriends, family members, best friends, have encouraged, paid for, and driven the get-away car for women seeking abortions. The pain of guilt runs deep and the scars are not healed. They cannot bear to behold the face of war that they have been so intimate in waging.

The face of war. It has the power to change those who gaze upon it in honest reflection. We, as a nation, must look squarely at the face of abortion, allow ourselves to be changed by it, and own up to our responsibility to stop it, or we will be doomed to remain trapped in the devastation of its bloody quagmire.

Appendix D

Why Supporting a Crisis Pregnancy Center is Not Enough

By Cheryl Sullenger

During pro-life outreaches to the churches we frequently run into perplexed Christians who cannot understand why we ask them to maintain a Christian testimony outside the local abortion clinics. Their chief defense against such action is that they support a crisis pregnancy center. This act, in their thinking, absolves them of any further responsibility in the matter of abortion. But does it?

The crisis pregnancy center's mission has evolved over the years since I first volunteered for one in the mid 1980's. At that time, unlike today, the centers saw many women who came in thinking the pro-life office was actually an abortion clinic. Using graphic images and a now-outdated video called "A Matter of Choice" many woman changed their minds about abortion and saved their babies.

As I worked at counseling women at a San Diego area crisis pregnancy center, or CPC, (now no longer in business), I was confronted one day by a tearful, angry woman. "Where were you when I needed you," she cried. "If you had been at the abortion clinic when I had my abortion, I would have kept my baby!" I realized she was attempting to shift the blame of her abortion onto me but I nevertheless became troubled at the fact that many more women than we could ever reach bypassed the CPC option and went straight to the abortion clinics. "What about these women?" I thought. Having had much success in changing the minds of truly abortion-minded women, I knew that if we took our counseling to the street in front of the abortion offices we could save even more lives.

I met a gentleman who did "sidewalk counseling" at the old WomanCare abortion clinic, then located in a rundown converted house in a homosexual neighborhood near downtown and decided to join him there. As we stood on the street trying to hand out pro-life brochures while dodging the homosexual clinic escorts, the police arrived and told us to move across the street or be arrested. This being my first time on the street and because I wanted to be a good witness to the police, I moved. Just then a couple came up to the abortion clinic. It was clear that the woman was distraught. I fidgeted on the street, unsure of what to do, especially with a police officer at my elbow trying to intimidate us into leaving. A few minutes after the couple went in, the woman emerged in tears. She had a clipboard with the abortion consent forms still in her hand. Her boyfriend followed her around the corner where she stood weeping. As I was about to call out to them the police officer told me I was not allowed to speak. I waited anxiously as I saw the boyfriend put his arm around her neck and forcibly drag her, still sobbing, into the mill. As this was happening the officer next to me said, "If you say one word you are going to jail." I did not speak, and the woman went inside and did not come out again while we were there.

I have felt an intense regret for putting my good reputation and personal safety above the life of that child and well-being of that poor woman. I learned a valuable lesson that day. I understood for the first time how vitally important the outreaches at the clinics are. Without Christians offering help to these women who fall through the CPC safety net, many women will abort who would not if they were given compassion and love when and where they needed it most. I promised that next time I would speak out on behalf of the woman and her child in obedience to Proverbs 31:8-9 and other scriptural mandates, then trust God to take care of me. Many have tried to make me stop this work, but I know that I must obey God in this matter, rather than man, be it a police officer or a misguided pastor.

Today, many in the churches want us to accept that supporting a CPC is enough and that they have no further responsibility in the matter of abortion. However, that excuse falls flat when we consider the thousands of women who will never take advantage of the CPCs, which today mostly offer their assistance to women who have already decided to carry their babies to term. **It is my estimate that approximately 1,000 abortions take place in San Diego County alone each _week_.** Now take into consideration the hundreds of communities in our nation where abortion clinics operate, and the numbers become staggering. Are we just to abandon these women to the hands of the abortionists only to come to their aid after the fact with "post-abortion counseling?" This is the equivalent of the priest and the Levite passing by on the other side of the road to avoid their responsibility to render aid to the beaten man. Jesus told us to follow instead the example of the Good Samaritan. Did the Samaritan simply pray for the beaten man when he returned to the comfortable confines of his local church? Did the Samaritan open an office where beaten and robbed people could make appointments for assistance? This sounds absurd, of course, but this is how the church has largely dealt with the matter of abortion.

The abandonment by the church of the women and their pre-born children scheduled to die at our local mills is an intolerable situation. The crisis pregnancy centers offer support to women who have decided to keep their babies, but the CPCs cannot reach the thousands of women **per week** who have scheduled to kill their babies at our country's abortion mills **nor are they designed to**. But sidewalk counselors and prayer teams can. The effectiveness of a peaceful Christian testimony at the mills is proven to save lives and change hearts.

However, we find often-hostile resistance from the pastors who intimidate their congregations into silence, thus bringing the bloodguilt of those aborted children they abandoned upon them and their congregations. Supporting a crisis pregnancy center, while admirable, is not enough. In the name of Christian Charity, let's stop treating these abortion-bound women and their babies like they do not exist or are not important and give them the same care, love, and meaningful assistance that we, as a Church, provide to those who have decided to give birth. Let us follow the example of the Good Samaritan, find the abortion site nearest us and, as Jesus said, "Go and do likewise."

Appendix E

Bible Study

Here is provided for you an outline for further study on the issues of innocent blood and bloodguilt.

1. **The shedding of innocent blood is murder.**

   a. Genesis 9:6: "Whoever sheds the blood of man, by man shall his blood be shed; for in the image of God has God made man. Whoever sheds the blood of man, by man shall his blood be shed; for in the image of God has God made man."

   b. Exodus 20:13: "You shall not murder" is the Sixth Commandment.

   c. Numbers 35:29-30: The death penalty for murder is not to be repealed.

   d. All killing is not murder
      1. Capital punishment is not murder, (Genesis 9:6-7; Romans 13:4)
      2. Self-Defense is not murder, (2 Samuel 2:18-23; 2 Chronicles 26:15)
      3. Just warfare is not murder, (Joshua 11:6; Psalm 144:1-2)

   e. Jesus death was innocent bloodshed, (Acts 7: 52-53)

f. Other examples of innocent bloodshed
      1. Abel, (Genesis 2:4-16)
      2. Uriah the Hittite, (2 Samuel 11:1-12:14)
      3. Naboth, (1 Kings 21:1-19)
      4. Deacon Steven, (Acts 7:54-60)

2. Innocent blood has a voice.

a. Genesis 4:10: Abel's voice cries from the ground in testimony against Cain.

b. Hebrews 12:22-24: Jesus' blood speaks a better word than that of Abel. Abel's blood cries for vengeance, Christ's for mercy.

c. Revelation 6:9-11: The murdered saints cry to God for vengeance.

3. What is Bloodguilt? It is the consequence of innocent bloodshed.

a. Deuteronomy 19:1-13, the Cities of Refuge: God goes out of His way to establish a judicial system so that innocent blood would not be shed in the land.

b. Jonah 1:4-16: Even the pagans turned to God at the understanding that taking part in a murder would bring the curse of bloodguilt.

c. Matthew 27 3-10: Judas hung himself because he was condemned for the bloodguilt he bore.

d. Act 5:25-28: The High Priest told Peter not to preach in the name of Christ because of the bloodguilt associated with Jesus' murder.

4. Bloodguilt affects more people than just the persons directly involved in the homicide.

    a.   Deuteronomy 21: The religious leaders and civil magistrates bear responsibility for justice. If they are unwilling to bear this responsibility, they share in the bloodguilt. God establishes a means of cleansing bloodguilt.

    b.   Matthew 23:29-36: The bloodguilt associated with murdering the prophets crossed generational lines and caused judgment to fall upon the land and people of Israel even though they did not personally commit the murders.

    c.   Matthew 27:25: The people demanded the blood of Jesus be accounted to them and their children.

5. Bloodguilt's circle of culpability.

    a.   Jeremiah 26:15: Outline the culpable parties.
        1. The murderers and the accomplices are culpable for innocent blood.
        2. The city or land is defiled by innocent blood.
        3. The inhabitants or populace bear bloodguilt when justice is not served.

    b.   Matthew 23:29-36: The bloodguilt of one generation can affect succeeding generations.

6. The murder of innocent children (including abortion) is especially condemned.

    a.   Leviticus 20:1-5: The Biblical injunction against

child-killing.

   b. 2 Kings 24:1-4: Judah is taken into captivity by
      Babylon in large part due to the shedding of
      innocent blood (child sacrifice) during the days
      of Manasseh.

   c. 2 Kings 21:1-6: Evidence of Manasseh's child-
      killing.

   d. Psalm 106:34-39: Israel's sin of child-killing
      recounted.

7. The result of bloodguilt is judgment.

   a. Ezekiel 9: Innocent bloodshed brings judgment
      to Israel and Judah.

   b. Ezekiel 22: Judgment promised to Judah for
      innocent bloodshed.

   c. Matthew 23:25: Jesus rebukes those hypocrites
      who shed the innocent blood of the prophets
      and warns of impending judgment.

   d. 2 Kings 21:1-6, 2 Kings 24:1-4: Judah judged
      for bloodshed that God would not forgive.

   e. Isaiah 1:15-20: Judgment for the shedding of
      innocent blood will come if there is no
      repentance.

8. The Church as a responsibility to maintain an attitude of repentance.

a. 1 Peter 4:17: Judgment begins in the house of God; His people are held to a high standard of culpability.

b. Revelation 2-3: Five out of the seven churches of Asia are told to repent.

c. Revelation 3:19: "As many as I love, I rebuke and chasten."

9. The Road to Restoration: Isaiah 1

a. Isaiah 1:1-15: National sin, including innocent bloodshed, is detailed.

b. Isaiah 1:16-20: Repentance is urged as a first step toward restoration.
    1. 2 Chronicles 7:14: Repentance will bring national healing
    2. Isaiah 1:18: Forgiveness is promised even for the sin of murder.

c. Isaiah 1:17a: Israel is encouraged to rebuke the wicked as a means of restoring justice.
    1. Ezekiel 3 and 33: God's people are charged with the duty of   watchmen.

d. Isaiah: 1:17b: Israel told to rescue the innocent as a fruit of repentance.
    1. Proverbs 24:11: The righteous must rescue those unjustly scheduled for death.
    2. Proverbs 31:8-9: Mandate to speak for the voiceless and defend the poor and needy.

3. Luke 10: 29-37: The Good Samaritan teaches sacrificially to render meaningful assistance to those in need.

e. Isaiah 1:18-19, 24-27: Restoration through justice promised.

10. Conclusion. Stopping abortion is the duty of every Christian and required for restoration.

a. The three principles of restoration, repenting, rebuking, and rescuing, need all to be followed with none ignored.

b. Isaiah 1:18: The crimsons stains are bloodstained hands. Only when we follow God's Word completely can we find our sins washed as white as snow.

Avenues of Application and Action

1. Consider taking time in prayer for introspection and personal repentance.

2. Make a commitment to regularly speak out against the wicked institution of abortion and take meaningful action to save innocent babies from abortion.

3. Recruit your friends and family to join you as you engage the defense of life in your community.

Other Resources from ORW

Am I Now Your Enemy for Telling You the Truth?
This short book answers frequently asked questions concerning the biblical doctine of bloodguilt and why the church must become actively involved in stopping abortion.

Bioethics in an Age of Emerging Biotechnology
Explains in simple terms the new technologies dominating today's headlines then deals with the ethics from a Biblical perspective.

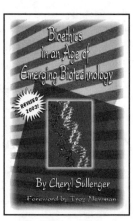

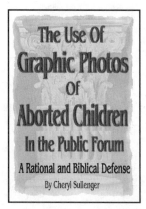

The Use of Graphic Photos in the Public Forum
This apologetic essay gives a Biblical defense for the public use of graphic pictures of aborted babies.

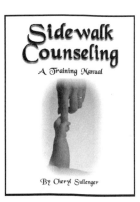

Sidewalk Counseling Manual
This "How-To" manual gives training and practical tips for Christians who reach out to women at the doors of the abortion mills.

Consider All the Consequences
Abortion's risks and consequences are clearly presented in this tri-fold brochure designed for use by sidewalk counselors.
Availible in English and Spanish.

For current prices or to order please contact:
Operation Rescue West
P.O. Box 601150, Sacramento, CA 95860
www.operationrescue.org